in their own words

Queen

Mick St. Michael

OMNIBUS PRESS

Edited by Chris Charlesworth
Cover & book designed by 4i Limited
Picture research by David Brolan

ISBN: 0.7119.3014.7
Order No.OP46879

Exclusive distributors:

Book Sales Limited,
8/9 Frith Street,
London W1V 5TZ, UK.

Music Sales Corporation,
257 Park Avenue South,
New York, NY 10010, USA.

Music Sales Pty Ltd,
120 Rothschild Avenue,
Rosebery, NSW 2018, Australia.

To the Music Trade only:

Music Sales Limited,
8/9 Frith Street,
London W1V 5TZ, UK.

Photo credits:
Front cover: London Features International
Back cover: London Features International (top);
    Rex Features (bottom).
Steve Double: page 101.
London Features International: 4, 6, 8, 9, 10, 11, 12, 14, 15,
    16, 17, 18, 20, 21, 22, 23, 24, 25, 26, 28, 29, 31, 36, 37, 38,
    39, 40, 41, 42, 44, 47, 48, 50, 51, 52, 53, 54, 55, 56, 57, 59,
    60, 62, 63, 65, 67, 68, 69, 70, 71, 72, 75, 76, 78, 81, 82, 85,
    86, 87, 88, 91, 92, 94, 95, 96, 97, 99, 100, 108 (top & bottom),
    109, 110, 111, 112.
Pictorial Press: 7, 19.
Press Association: 107.
Rex Features: 3, 13, 27, 30, 32, 33, 34, 35, 43, 45, 46, 49, 58,
    61, 64, 73, 74, 77, 79, 80, 83, 84, 89, 93, 102, 103, 104,
    105, 106, 108 (centre).

Printed in Great Britain by
Scotprint Ltd., Musselburgh

Every effort has been made to trace the copyright holders of
the photographs in this book but one or two were unreachable.
We would be grateful if the photographers concerned would
contact us.

A catalogue record for this book is available from the British
Library.

Contents

Introduction

Queen achieved legendary status long before Freddie Mercury, their ebullient lead singer, died from pneumonia complicated by AIDS in November 1991. Three months later the audience at the Brits awards ceremony at Hammersmith Odeon and millions more watching their television sets at home witnessed Brian May and Roger Taylor, Queen's media spokesmen for the past decade, receive an award for the best British single during the evening's emotional highlight. This was for the reissued 'Bohemian Rhapsody' which topped the charts for the second time over Christmas 1991 amid a wave of public sympathy and, ironically, the best press the group had ever enjoyed during their 20 year career.

How different this was from the early days, when the rock press damned them as pretentious latecomers to the glam-rock party or hyped upstarts whose lack of pedigree was equalled only by their lack of taste. The concept of rock with a sense of humour was as alien to the progressive era of 1972 as Queen would be irrelevant to the new wave that five years later swept rock's dinosaurs clean away. The difference was that by 1977 Queen had reached a plateau of critical approbation that rendered them in a class of their own.

Bass player John Deacon, the last of the four members to join, is a man of few words who let the music speak for him. His most memorable pronouncements concerned Live Aid, the 1985 event at which Queen distinguished themselves most honourably and which clearly moved him far more than success, wealth and fame. Roger and Brian, ever ready to be interviewed, were always keen to discuss their music while Freddie, after delighting the media with a succession of outrageous quotes, shut up shop as far as interviews were concerned in the mid Eighties. His pronouncements from then until his untimely death were few and far between but always worth hearing. Sadly, many of his earlier remarks made in semi-jest about his sexual appetite and preferences would, in retrospect, seem particularly tragic. But Freddie knew what his public expected. "Art… showbiz… they want to see you rush off in your limousine." Humorous self-mockery was always part of the act.

From the beginning, Queen went their own set way. Heroes of Live Aid, they played the South African resort of Sun City mere months later, ending up as villains on the UN blacklist. At a time when superstar live acts were in short supply, they retired from touring. They hitched their wagon to a number of powerful managers, then opted to manage themselves. Their clip for 'Bohemian Rhapsody' started the video revolution – yet was shot on a whim and cost less than £5,000. Musically, they refused to be pigeonholed: two US chart-topping singles, the rockabilly flavoured 'Crazy Little Thing Called Love' and the funky 'Another One Bites The Dust' actually came from the same album.

Throughout it all, however, the media – and especially the rock press – refused to take them seriously. Only Freddie's death, as rock's first major Aids casualty, brought forth the tributes that were lacking during his lifetime. The dignity of his departure contrasted strongly with the flamboyance of his public persona, but that was just one more of the many paradoxes that had surrounded Queen from the earliest days.

There was never any question of their carrying on without their figurehead – yet as this book shows, the band was made up of four quite distinct individuals, the sum total of whose parts added up to a rock legend. By letting the quartet speak for themselves, Queen In Their Own Words comes as close as any other book to revealing what made them tick.

Pre-Queen

"None of the groups really got anywhere because we never played any real gigs or took it that seriously."
Brian

"1984 was purely an amateur band, formed at school, although perhaps at the end we once got fifteen quid or something. We never really played anything significant in the way of original material – it was a strange mixture of cover versions, all the things which people wanted to hear at the time. This was about the time that The Stones were emerging, and later we did Stones and Yardbirds things – I was in the band for a couple of years, although it wasn't very serious – we did a few dances and things, but I was never happy about it. I left because I wanted to do something where we wrote our own material.

"I advertised on a notice board at college for a drummer, because by this time, Cream and Hendrix were around, and I wanted a drummer who could handle that sort of stuff, and Roger was easily capable of it. Tim Staffell, who had been in in 1984, was our singer, and we formed this group called Smile, which was semi-pro. We travelled around the country a fair bit, as far as Cornwall and Liverpool, and although we did well in some places, we never felt we were getting anywhere, because if you don't have a record out, people tend to forget who you are very quickly, even if they like you on the night."
Brian

"I could play you tapes of Smile which have the same general structures to what we're doing today."
Brian (1977)

Early Days

**"Why are you wasting your time doing this?
You should do more original material. You should be more
demonstrative in the way that you put the music across.
If I was your singer that's what I'd be doing!"**

Freddie (to Brian and Roger in 1970)

"Freddie was a friend of Tim Staffell's and came along to a lot of our gigs, and offered suggestions in a way that couldn't be refused! At that time, he hadn't really done any singing, and we didn't know he could – we thought he was just a theatrical rock musician."
Brian

"Smile completely broke up, and we gave up – Freddie was the driving force for getting us back together. He told us we could do it, and said he didn't want to play useless gigs where no-one listened, and that we would have to rehearse and get a stage act together –he was very keen for it to be an actual act – and we started again, taking a couple of songs from Smile and a couple of songs from groups he'd been in, like a band called Wreckage from which we stole bits that went into 'Liar' and a couple of other songs, and we set about it in a serious manner. We'd rehearse three or four nights a week in places like lecture theatres, and we managed to scrape together some equipment."
Brian

"Even in the beginning when we couldn't afford a light show, we used projector lamps for lights, and we just got through somehow, getting someone to drive us, or borrowing a bigger van – it was scraping through all the way."
Brian (1983)

"If we were going to drop the careers we'd trained hard for we wanted to make a really good job of music. We all had quite a bit to lose, really, and it didn't come easy. To be honest, I don't think any of us realized it would take a full three years to get anywhere. It was certainly no fairy tale."
Brian (1971)

"We said okay, we're going to take the plunge into rock and we're really going to do a job at it, no half measures. We all had potentially good careers and we weren't prepared to settle for second best if we were going to abandon all the qualifications we had got in other fields."
Freddie

"Our stage act was a show, more rock'n'roll oriented than the album, actually, at that stage of the game. You can only get so far in playing to audiences who don't understand what you're doing, so we did more heavy rock'n'roll with the Queen delivery to give people something they could get hold of – get on, sock it to 'em, get off! If you go on stage and people don't know your material, you can get boring if you do your own stuff all the time. So we did Bo Diddley's 'I'm A Man', Elvis Presley's 'Jailhouse Rock' and Little Richard's 'Shout Bama Lama'. Give 'em a show, but don't make anything but the music your foundation."
Brian (1972)

"I was possibly the one person in the group who could look at it from the outside, because I came in as the fourth person in the band. I knew there was something there but I wasn't convinced of it… until possibly the 'Sheer Heart Attack' album."
John (1971)

"We did have a bass player, and we went through a few of them, but either the personality or the musical ability didn't fit, and it was a while before we found John, through some friends. We used to call him Deacon John, and it appeared like that on the first album, but after that, he objected to it, and said he wanted to be called John Deacon. I don't really know why we called him Deacon John in the first place – just one of those silly things."
Brian (1983)

"We thought Roger was the best drummer we'd ever seen. I watched him tuning a snare – something I'd never seen done before – and I remember thinking how professional he looked."
Brian (1971)

"I did have one real contact, a guy called Terry who was working at the time for Pye Studios, but was moving to the new De Lane Lea studios, and he said they needed people in there to make some noise, because they were testing the separation between the three studios, and the reverberation times, and they wanted a group to do it. Roy Thomas Baker came to De Lane Lea, completely by accident, as far as I know, and said that he liked what we were doing very much, and I think it was through him recommending us to Trident that they finally gave us a contract."
Brian (1983)

"For the first two years nothing really happened. We were all studying, but progress in the band was nil. We had great ideas, though, and somehow I think we all felt we'd get through."
Roger

The Music

"I'm just a musical prostitute, my dear!"
Freddie

"We've been compared to Alice Cooper, Rod Stewart, Led Zeppelin, Deep Purple – everybody. There must be parallels, but we were not aware of them. Obviously we have our heroes. I personally think Zeppelin and The Who are the two best bands in the world. I've got all their albums and I've listened to them a lot. I still think John Bonham is one of the most underrated rock drummers so I suppose we've absorbed some of that somewhere."
Roger (1974)

"We don't especially go out to play heavy music or light music – it's just our kind of music."
Brian (1974)

"Def Leppard once asked me how we got our vocal sound, did we use hundreds of tracks all the time?

"It's more like six usually. Apart from Freddie's leads, it's from him, Roger and me singing lines in unison. Fred has this sharp crystal tone, Roger is husky and raw, and I have a sort of roundness. Put them together, double-track it, and it comes out big."
Brian (1991)

"Sparks are a single minded band who are progressing along one track, while I think Queen are also progressing but in a different way. I think we are interesting in trying a lot of different things."
Brian (1974)

"We're not a singles group. We don't stake our reputation on singles and we never have done, but I think it's brought in a lot of younger people to our concerts."
Brian

"I'm into paradoxes. I wanted to make an album about them, but the group told me I was a pretentious fart. They were right."
Brian (1981)

"My songs are like Bic razors. For fun, for modern consumption. You listen to it, like it, discard it, then on to the next. Disposable pop."
Freddie

"We did some John Peel sessions for the BBC, and a lot of people thought we used synthesizers, so we wanted to make sure people knew it was all guitars and voices – I think that for the first nine albums we made there was never a synthesizer and never an orchestra, never any other player except us on the records."
Brian (1983)

"I write commercial love songs because basically what I feel very strongly about is love and emotion. I'm not a John Lennon who sleeps in bags for I don't know how long. You have to have a certain upbringing and go through a certain amount of history before people will believe what you're writing about."
Freddie

"People may not generally admit it, but I think when most people write songs, there's more than one level to them – they'll be about one thing on the surface, but underneath, they're probably trying, maybe even unconsciously, to say something about their own life, their own experience – and in nearly all my stuff, there's a personal feeling."
Brian

"I'm quite aware of what's going on, but that doesn't mean that I want to incorporate trends into our songs. I write a song the way I feel it, and if that means bringing in something old-fashioned, I'll do that. I will never let the song down."
Freddie

"I love heavy metal and I don't look down on it at all. But we're not a heavy metal group, so if we do it I guess there has to be a consciousness in there. I love AC/DC, it's very pure. But we're not that way, so we can't pretend we are. It's good to be able to step back and see the funny side of it, 'cos it kicks out some of the shit."
Brian (1989)

"It would be bloody ludicrous if Queen made a record using Acid House techniques. It would be jumping on bandwagons and we've never been ones for that."
Roger (1989)

"I like to live with the song for a while without touching the guitar at all. Then I can form an idea in my head of what I'd like to play and then work it out on the guitar and take it into the studio pretty much complete."
Brian (1990)

The Albums & Songs

"On the first few albums the songs would grow into strange shapes."

Brian

'Queen'

"There were lots of things on the first album I don't like, for example the drum sound. There are parts of it which may sound contrived but it is very varied and it has lots of energy."
Roger (1974)

"'Queen' sold really well over a longish period and coincided with our breaking ground concertwise. So we really had matured as a group and had our audience before the press caught on to us. I think that actually gave us a better start because we were better prepared."
Brian (1977)

"The album took ages and ages – two years in total, in the preparation, making and then trying to get the thing released."
Brian

'My Fairy King'
"This was the first time we'd really seen Freddie working at his full capacity. He's virtually a self–taught pianist, and he was making vast strides at the time, although we didn't have a piano on stage at that point because it would have been impossible to fix up. So in the studio was the first chance Freddie had to do his piano things, and we actually got that sound of the piano and guitar working for the first time, which was very exciting. 'My Fairy King' was the first of these sort of epics where there were lots of voice overdubs and harmonies. Freddie got into (this), and that led to 'The March Of The Black Queen' on the second album, and then 'Bohemian Rhapsody' later on."
Brian

'Queen II'

"We took so much trouble over that album, possibly too much, but when we finished we felt really proud. Immediately it got really bad reviews, so I took it home to listen to and thought Christ, are they right? But after hearing it a few weeks later I still like it. I think it's great. We'll stick by it."
Roger (1974)

"For some strange reason we seemed to get rather a different feel on the album because of the way we were forced to record it, and even allowing for the problems we had none of us were really displeased with the final result."
Brian

"Considering the abuse we've had latterly I'm surprised that the new LP had done so well. I suppose it's basically that audiences like the band."
Roger (1974)

"Led Zeppelin and The Who are probably in there somewhere because they were among our favourite groups, but what we were trying to do differently from either of those groups was this sort of layered sound. The Who had the open chord guitar sound, and there's a bit of that in 'Father To Son', but our sound is more based on the overdriven guitar sound, which is used for the main bulk of the song, but I also wanted to build up textures behind the main melody lines. To me, 'Queen II' was the sort of emotional music we'd always wanted to be able to play, although we couldn't play most of it on stage because it was too complicated...

"We were trying to push studio techniques to a new limit for rock groups – it was fulfilling all our dreams because we didn't have much opportunity for that on the first album. It went through our minds to call the album 'Over The Top'."
Brian

'Sheer Heart Attack'

"I have the feeling that the whole thing is getting a bit more professional all round. We are, after all, on our third album."
John (1974)

"With 'Sheer Heart Attack', I was able to see the group from the outside, and was pretty excited by what I saw. We'd done a few things before I was ill, but when I came back they'd done a load more, including a couple of backing tracks of songs by Freddie which I hadn't heard like 'Flick Of The Wrist', which excited me and gave me a lot of inspiration to get back in there and do what I wanted to do. I also managed to do some writing – 'Now I'm Here' was done in that period. That song's about experiences on the American tour, which really blew me away. I was bowled over by the amazing aura which surrounds rock music in America.

"'Brighton Rock' showed how my style was evolving, particularly with the solo bit in the middle, which I'd been doing on the Mott The

Hoople tour and has gradually expanded ever since. That involved using the repeat device in time with an original guitar phrase, which I don't think had been done before.

"We weren't going for hits, because we always thought of ourselves as an album group, but we did think that perhaps we'd dished up a bit too much for people to swallow on 'Queen II'."
Brian

"I've got more confidence in the group now than ever before. I was possibly the one person in the group who could look at it from the outside because I was the fourth person in the band. I knew there was something there but I wasn't so convinced of it. Till possibly this album."
John (1974)

'Killer Queen'
"People are used to hard rock, energy music from Queen, yet with this single, you almost expect Noël Coward to sing it. It's one of those bowler hat, black suspender belt numbers – not that Noël Coward would wear that."
Freddie

"It was the turning point. It was the song that best summed up our kind of music, and a big hit, and we desperately needed it as a mark of something successful happening for us. We were penniless, you know, just like any other struggling rock'n'roll band. All sitting around London in bedsitters, just like the rest."
Brian (1974)

"It's about a high class call girl. I'm trying to say that classy people can be whores as well. That's what the song is about, though I'd prefer people to put their own interpretation upon it – to read what they like into it."
Freddie

"A lot of people thought we were just a heavy metal group but 'Killer Queen' showed a completely new side to the band. Certainly the album bridges the gap – it's more listenable and will appeal to more people."
John (1974)

'A Night At The Opera'

"I think we knew we had something special. We said, 'This can be our Sgt Pepper. Or whatever'.
    "We ran the tape through so many times it kept wearing out. Once we held the tape up to the light and we could see straight through it, the music had practically vanished. We transferred it in a hurry. Strange business – holding on to this elusive sound signal which gradually disappeared as we created it. Every time Fred decided to add a few more 'Galileos' we lost something too."
Brian (1991)

"There were a lot of things we needed to do on 'Queen II' and 'Sheer Heart Attack' but there wasn't space enough. This time there is. Guitarwise and on vocals we've done things we've never done before.
    "To finish the album we will work till we are legless. I'll sing until my throat is like a vulture's crotch. We haven't even reached the halfway stage yet but from the things I can hear we have surpassed everything we've done before musically."
Freddie (1975)

"'The Prophet's Song' had been around for quite a long time, and I finished the lyrics off when we were making this album. I don't know exactly what inspired the words – I had a dream

about some of it, which I put into the song.
    "With 'Good Company', I indulged a little fetish of mine - all the things that sound like other instruments, like trumpets and clarinets, were done with guitar. To get the effect of the instruments, I was doing one note at a time with the pedal and building them up, so you can imagine how long it took. There was such a wide variety on those albums – Fred doing a really quite slushy ballad, then a heavy rock thing, then something else – and we were willing to try everything because we always wanted to expand our range."
Brian

"'39' is a science fiction story about someone who goes away and leaves his family, and because of the time-dilation effect, where the people on earth have aged a lot more than he has when he returns, he's aged a year and they've aged a hundred years – I felt a little like that about my home at the time, having been away and seen this vastly different world of rock music, which was totally different from the way I was brought up."
Brian

'Bohemian Rhapsody'

"'Bohemian Rhapsody' didn't just come out of thin air. I did a bit of research, although it was tongue in cheek and it was a mock opera. Why not? I certainly wasn't saying I was an opera fanatic and I knew everything about it."
Freddie (1975)

"People used to have clips before, but they were often shot on film. It was quite accidental… at the time we were touring England, and we knew we wouldn't be able to get to record Top Of The Pops on the Wednesday. Our managers at the time had a mobile unit, so it was actually shot on video, in about four hours!"
John (1975)

"A lot of people slammed 'Bohemian Rhapsody', but who can you compare that to? Name one group that's done an operatic single. We were adamant that 'Bohemian Rhapsody' could be a hit in its entirety. We have been forced to make compromises, but cutting up a song will never be one of them!"
Freddie (1975)

"We wanted to experiment with sound. Sometimes we used three studios simultaneously. 'Bohemian Rhapsody' took bloody ages to record but we had all the freedom we wanted and we've been able to go to greater extremes."
Freddie (1975)

"'Rhapsody' is not a stage number. A lot of people don't like us leaving the stage. But to be honest, I'd rather leave than have us playing to a backing tape. If you're out there and you've got backing tapes, it's a totally false situation.

"So we'd rather be up front about it and say, 'Look, this is not something you can play on stage. It was multi-layered in the studio. We'll play it because we think you want to hear it.' We're not into the over the top production for the sake of it but because it highlights the music, that's the object in our eyes."
Brian (1979)

"Everyone thought that the film was a huge production, but it was actually shot in only four hours. It was really easy to do, and since then we've spent a lot of time on films that probably weren't as good and certainly didn't get the exposure."
Brian (1979)

"'Bohemian Rhapsody' was really Freddie's baby from the beginning: he came in and knew exactly what he wanted. The backing track was done with just piano, bass and drums, with a few spaces for other things to go in, like the tic-tic-tic on the hi-hat to keep the time, and Freddie sang a guide vocal at the time, but he had all his harmonies written out, and it was really just a question of doing it."
Brian

"People like Jonathan King have made lots of money through writing crass rubbish B-sides to decent songs. But I can talk – I wrote the B-side to 'Bohemian Rhapsody'; mind you, that was a good song. In effect, I made just as much money then as Freddie did for writing 'Bohemian Rhapsody', which people bought the record for. That's not right, is it? But justice and the law are two different things."
Roger (1990)

'A Day At The Races'

"I wish in some ways that we had put 'A Night At The Opera' and 'A Day At The Races' out together, because the material for both of them was more or less written at the same time, and it corresponds to an almost exactly similar period in our development, so I regard the two albums as completely parallel, and the fact that one came out after the other is a shame, because it was looked on as a follow-up, whereas really it was sort of an extension of the first one."
Brian

'News Of The World'

"'Sleeping On The Sidewalk' was the quickest song I've ever written – I just wrote it down, and I'm quite pleased with it as well, because it's not highly subtle, but it leaves me with a good feeling. It was the sort of thing any guitarist who had played a bit of blues would do, and I could very well have had Eric Clapton in the back of my mind. It was a one-take thing as well – so it has a kind of sloppy feel, but that works with the song.

"I suppose 'It's Late' is as close to typical

Queen as you can get, and there's a kind of style in there, which I've often thought about, which is somewhere between my kind of thing on 'It's Late', and one of Freddie's, something like 'We Are The Champions'. It's so easy for us to do, and we can slip into it almost without thinking, on stage and on record. Once Freddie starts playing E flat and A flat on the piano, which he very often does, it has a particular sound… (that) produces something different out of me."
Brian

'We Are The Champions'

"That song 'We Are The Champions' has been taken up by football fans because it's a winners' song. I can't believe that someone hasn't written a new song to overtake it."
Freddie (1985)

"I can understand some people saying 'We Are The Champions' was bombastic. But it wasn't saying Queen are the champions, it was saying all of us are. It made the concert like a football match, but with everyone on the same side."
Brian (1991)

'Jazz'

"We thought it would be nice to try again with a producer (Roy Thomas Baker) on whom we could put some of the responsibility. We'd found a few of our own methods, and so had he, and on top of what we'd collectively learned before, we thought that coming back together would mean that there would be some new stuff going on, and it worked pretty well.

"It was just a bit of fun really – we thought the two songs ('Fat Bottomed Girls' and 'Bicycle Race') went together, and the album was sort of European flavoured. We'd never recorded in Europe, and we absorbed some of the feeling."
Brian

'Bicycle Race'/'Fat Bottomed Girls'

"We lost some of our audience with that. 'How could you do it? It doesn't go with your spiritual side'. But my answer is that the physical side is just as much a part of a person as the spiritual or intellectual side. It's fun. I'll make no apologies. All music skirts around sex, sometimes very directly. Ours doesn't. In our music, sex is either implied or referred to semi-jokingly, but it's always there."
Brian (1978)

'Live Killers'

"Live albums are inescapable, really – everyone tells you you have to do them, and when you do, you find that they're very often not of mass appeal, and in the absence of a fluke condition you sell your live album to the converted, the people who already know your stuff and come to the concerts. So if you add up the number of people who've seen you over the last few years, that's very roughly the number who'll buy your live album unless you have a hit single on it, which we didn't.

"That's a harmoniser thing (on 'Get Down, Make Love') which I've used really as a noise more than a musical thing. It's controllable because I had a special little pedal made for it, which means I can change the interval at which the harmoniser comes back, and it's fed back on itself so it makes all swooping noises. It's just an exercise in using that together with noises from Freddie – a sort of erotic interlude."
Brian

'The Game'

"Recently, we've become more selective, I think, and we try to make albums which don't go in so many directions at once – for example, 'The Game' album was really pruned, and the others refused to include a couple of things I wanted on, because they said they were too far outside the theme of the album, and

that we should be trying to make a slightly more coherent album."
Brian

"We approached that from a different angle, with the idea of ruthlessly pruning it down to a coherent album rather than letting our flights of fancy lead us off into different ideas. The impetus came very largely from Freddie, who said that he thought we'd been diversifying so much that people didn't know what we were about any more. If there's a theme to the album, it's rhythm and sparseness – never two notes played if one would do, which is a hard discipline for us, because we tend to be quite over the top in the way we work. So the whole thing has a very economical feel to it – a very modern sounding album."
Brian

"That was breaking new ground for us because for the first time we went into a recording studio without a deadline, purely with the intention of putting some tracks down as they came out. 'Crazy Little Thing Called Love' was one of them, another was 'Save Me'. There was a wide variety of things, and we're left in the position of having something in the can that we don't have to release straight away, and which at some future date we can perhaps fashion into an album.

"The basic reason for doing it was to put ourselves in a totally different situation. It's a way of getting out of that rut of doing an album, touring Britain, touring America, etc. We thought we'd try a change and see what came out. You have to make your own excitement after a while."
Brian

"Roger's really the guy who introduced us to synthesizers. You can now get polyphonic synths with a device for bending the notes which is much closer to the feel of a guitar than ever before, so now we use the synth, but sparingly, I think, particularly on 'The Game'. There's very little there, and what there is merely complements what we'd used already, so there's no danger of the synth taking over, which I would never allow to happen. I get a good feeling from playing the guitar which you don't get with anything else – a feeling of power, and a type of expression."
Brian

'Crazy Little Thing Called Love'
"We're not a singles group, we don't stake our reputation on singles and we never have done, but I think it's brought a lot of younger people to our concerts.

"No doubt there are those who hate the new single but like what we've done in the past. But I think that tends to happen with whatever you put out, unless you're totally predictable. You lose some and gain some. But the actual live show gives a good crossover, so I don't think anyone's disappointed with that."
Brian (1979)

"I wrote it in the bath. I actually dragged an upright piano to my bedside once. I've been known to scribble lyrics in the middle of the night without putting the light on."
Freddie

"It's not rockabilly exactly, but it did have that early Elvis feel, and it was one of the first records to exploit that. In fact I read somewhere – in Rolling Stone I think it was – that John Lennon heard it and it gave him the impetus to start recording again. If it's true – and listening to the last album it certainly sounds as if he explored similar influences – that's wonderful."
Roger

"'Crazy Little Thing Called Love' was very untypical playing for me. I'd never used a Telecaster on record before, and a Boogie amplifier, which I'd never have considered using. It's a very sparse record, and it was done with Elvis Presley in mind, obviously – I thought that Freddie sounded a bit like Elvis, but somebody's done a cover of it who sounds absolutely like Elvis, and the whole record sounds like a Jordanaires/Elvis recreation."
Brian

'Another One Bites The Dust'
"I listened to a lot of soul music when I was in school and I've always been interested in that sort of music. I'd been wanting to do a track like 'Another One Bites The Dust' for a while, but originally all I had was the line and the bass riff.

Gradually I filled it in and the band added ideas.
I could hear it as a song for dancing but had no
idea it would become as big as it did. The song
got picked up off our album and some of the
black radio stations in the US started playing it,
which we've never had before."
John (1980)

"A lot of people have used 'Another One Bites
The Dust' as a theme song – the Detroit Lions
used it for their games, and they soon began to
lose, so they bit the dust soon afterwards, but it
was a help to the record – and there's been a few
cover versions of various kinds, notably
'Another One Rides The Bus', which is an
extremely funny record by a bloke called Mad
Al or something, in the States – it's hilarious. We
like people covering our songs in any way, no
matter what spirit it's done in, because it's great
to have anyone use your music as a base, a big
compliment."
Brian

'Flash Gordon'

"We'd been offered a few (soundtracks), but
most of them were where the film is written
around music, and that's been done to death –
it's the cliché of 'movie star appears in movie
about movie star' but this one (Flash Gordon)
was different in that it was a proper film and had
a real story which wasn't based around music,
and we would be writing a film score in the way
anyone else writes a film score – we were writing
to a discipline for the first time ever."
Brian

"We saw 20 minutes of the finished film and
thought it was very good and over the top… We
wanted to do something that was a real
soundtrack… It's a first in many ways, because a
rock group hasn't done this type of thing before,
or else it's been toned down and they've been
asked to write pretty mushy background music,
whereas we were given the licence to do what we
liked, as long as it complemented the picture."
Brian

'Hot Space'

"It is an attempt to do funk properly. It has a style of playing where you get in and get out quickly, hence the title 'Hot Space'."
Brian (1982)

"I think 'Hot Space' was a mistake, if only timing-wise. We got heavily into funk and it was quite similar to what Michael Jackson did on 'Thriller' a couple of years later and the timing was wrong. Disco was a dirty word."
Brian (1989)

"We would experiment with the rhythm and the bass and drum track and get that sounding right, and then very cautiously piece the rest around it, which was an experimental way for us to do it. In one track called 'Backchat', there wasn't going to be a guitar solo, because John Deacon, who wrote the song, has gone perhaps more violently black than the rest of us. We had lots of arguments about it, and what he was heading for in his tracks was a totally non-compromise situation, doing black stuff as R&B artists would do it with no concessions to our methods at all, and I was trying to edge him back towards the central path and get a bit of heaviness into it, and a bit of the anger of rock music. So one night I said I wanted to see what I could add to it – I felt that the song as it stood wasn't aggressive enough – it's 'Backchat', and it's supposed to be about people arguing and it should have some kind of guts to it. He agreed, and I went in and tried a few things."
Brian

"Possibly Fred was then getting interested in other things, and a bit bored with being in the studio, because we did studios to death with the previous two albums, when we'd be in there for months on end, just working away, although we weren't particularly inefficient, it was just that there was a lot to be done. We all felt we'd done enough of that for the time being, and wanted to get back to basics and do something simpler, but Fred got to the point where he could hardly stand being in a studio, and he'd want to do his bit and get out."
Brian (1983)

'Under Pressure'

"It's one of the very best things Queen have ever done, and it happened so casually, when David simply visited us at our studio in Montreux. As long as we can continue to do this, and surprise even ourselves, we'll carry on."
Roger (1981)

"David Bowie lives near the studio we bought in a little town close to Montreux, and when we were there, he'd often come over to see us, to chat and have a drink. Someone suggested that we should all go into the studio and play around one night, to see what came out – which we did, playing each other's old songs and just fiddling around. The next night, we listened to the tapes, because we'd left the tape recorder running, and picked out a couple of pieces which seemed to be promising, and then we just worked on one particular idea, which became 'Under Pressure', for a whole night – an extremely long night."
Brian

'The Works'

"I think our new album is damn good, much better than anything we've done for a while. It's going to be called 'The Works'. And it really is! There's all the Queen trademarks. Lots of production, arrangements and harmonies. We've experimented a lot in the past and some of the experiments didn't work. Our last album was one big experiment and a lot of people totally hated it. And it didn't sell very well – not compared to earlier stuff, anyway."
Brian

"I always got the most enjoyment out of the harder material. Actually, our new album is a lot harder… but I did fight to get it that way. We've done some fantastic over the top harmonies and a lot of heavy things that we haven't done for years.

"The pressure has always been against me, because not everybody in the band is into the same stuff as I am. I get the most pleasure out of things that I can hammer down and get some excitement out of. Basically, I'm like a little boy with the guitar, I just like the fat, loud sound of it. But that's not important to the others, and I agree with this, the songs come first. That's where the common ground ends and the arguments begin. The result is always a compromise."
Brian

'Radio Ga Ga'
"I'm an instinctive musician. I can play keyboards, guitar and drums and I can write songs. I have a facility for writing music, but I don't want to know anything particularly technical - like what the chords are called. Even in 'Radio Ga Ga' there are some very difficult chords – I don't know what they're called, but it doesn't matter. I'm a much better guitarist than I am a keyboard player, but now I find melodically it's much easier to write on keyboard. 'Radio Ga Ga' was a completely keyboard-written song. I defy anyone to write that on the guitar because you wouldn't find the chords – they wouldn't come naturally to any guitar player I know."
Roger

"One day the radio came on in our house and my three year old son Felix came out with 'Radio Poo Poo'! I thought that sounded good, so I changed it around a bit and came up with 'Radio Ga Ga'. The song came after I'd locked myself in a studio for three days with a synthesizer and a drum machine."
Roger

'I Want To Break Free'
"When we did the 'I Want To Break Free' video in drag, everyone in England thought it was very funny, but America hated it and looked on it as some gross insult."
Brian

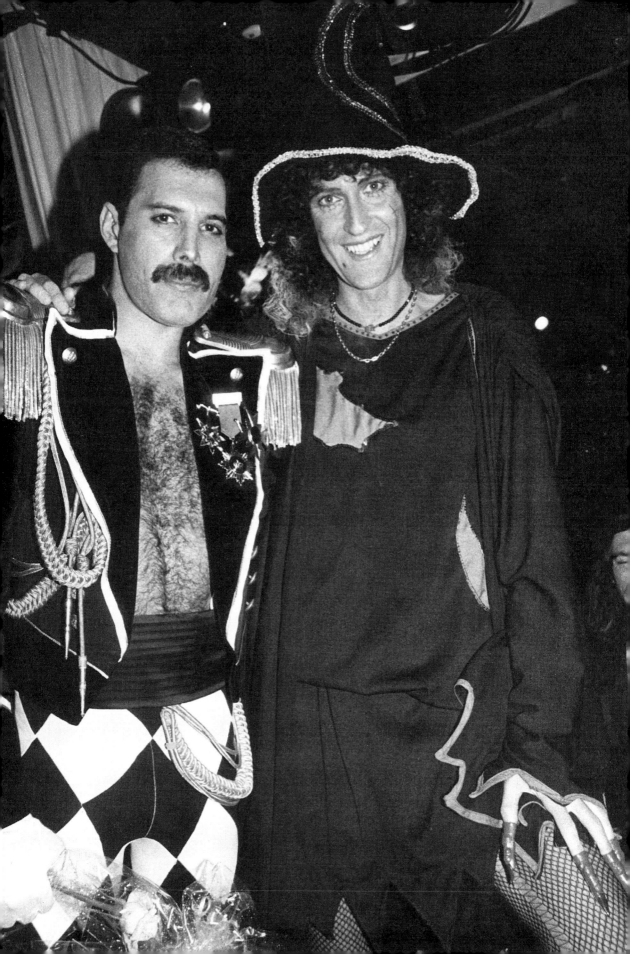

'A Kind Of Magic'

"'A Kind Of Magic' was specifically written for Russ Mulcahy's film Highlander. 'It's a kind of magic' was a line of Christopher Lambert's that I took from the film.

"I think the next album will be more of a unit. We're developing a tremendously powerful style – in rehearsal anyway – of playing together. I think it'll be more dramatic, more intense."
Roger

'One Vision'
"We do a lot of stuff for charities, but 'One Vision' was a way of getting back to what we're doing, and if we didn't run ourselves as a business we wouldn't be around for the next Live Aid. We're not in the full-time business of charity at all. We're in the business of making music, which is a good enough end in itself."
Brian

'The Miracle'
"It was OK, but we had our various fisticuffs."
Freddie (1989)

"We wanted to record a really democratic album, and each one of us would be involved in the songwriting. The consequence was that no-one was only partially involved, because each track was credited to all four musicians. Regardless of who had the basic idea for a song, we were all involved and worked on it to the same extent. So we created a real band feeling without any ego problems. That's also one of the reasons that 'The Miracle' has turned into such a better album than 'A Kind Of Magic', for example."
Brian

"I expect the press to say we're an arrogant bunch of bastards like they always do. 'The Miracle' isn't supposed to be us, it's supposed to be something that we're looking for – peace on earth – and that'll be lambasted as crass idealism. But there you go?"
Brian

"I think a lot of people really missed the typical Queen sound on our last few releases. 'The Miracle' includes all of Queen's typical elements in concentrated form. If you listen carefully, you can hear all the built-in references to our past albums."
Roger

"I think 'Kashoggi's Ship' and 'Was It All Worth It' are the two ends of the album, and both are comments on ourselves. We read about that kind of society life – the excess – we feel we've touched on those areas at some time… we've been through it."
Brian (1989)

"'I Want It All' re-establishes our old image in a way. It's nice to come back with something strong. Something that reminds people we're a live group.

"I don't think we're a singles band really. Just before we put the single out I started listening to what's on the radio, and the kind of stuff that becomes a hit these days bears no resemblance to what we do. People only remember the hits, but I suppose we have done OK."
Brian

"We've got a long break behind us, and had a lot of time to have a good think about things. All of a sudden the old energy was just there again. We badly wanted to play together again and write new songs. There's a certain magic in the air when we meet, because the chemistry within the band is just right! We're all working on various solo projects as well, but I don't think any of us would be able to produce an album like 'The Miracle' by themselves. Queen is still a special kind of band and not easy to replace for any of us – even though one could theoretically gain the same kind of success as a solo artist. When we met to work on the new material, we spent the first three weeks just playing together. We only had drums, guitar, bass, vocals and keyboards – the classic line-up.

"That's how everything started. And that's basically how everything's stayed. Maybe that's the reason why 'The Miracle' sounds more original and real. We left our egos outside the studio door and worked together as a real band, something that wasn't always the case with Queen. There were times when each one of us was only into his own compositions, and hardly contributed any ideas to any other songs. We didn't have any problems like that this time. We really enjoyed the production, that's why 'The Miracle' has turned into a real Queen album."
Brian

"A live video presentation of 'The Miracle' is a possibility. It was suggested the other day and we all loved the idea. We might create a mythical venue for it – the Miracle Pavilion. Out of that, hopefully, might come an idea for touring."
Roger (1989)

'Innuendo'

"We started writing the album about nine months ago. We went to Switzerland, where we have our own little studio, and worked there with co-producer Dave Richards for a couple of weeks just to see what came out. That's usually what we do. We often find it's very good to play together without too many fixed ideas to begin with. We very seldom have a lot of material when we go into the studio – there's ideas but they don't actually get formed until we get to work on it. We usually have two or three days just playing, finding sounds, getting the feel of each other again. We keep the multi-track running and seem to find that there's little bits that really seem to gel.

"It's quite a complex album. Some of the tracks are more along the lines of the mid-period stuff we did, like 'A Night At The Opera', where there's a lot of overdubs and complexity. It just takes a long time – you can't take short cuts. But it nearly killed me, because I was working on the other stuff as well, doing the music for the stage production of Macbeth.

"'Innuendo' is the title track, and that was one of the first things that came – it's got the bolero-type rhythm, a very strange track. That's going to be the first single here. It's a bit of a risk, but it's different, and you either win it all or you lose it all. It had a nice sound and feel, and we stuck with that.

"'Innuendo' was gradually evolved by the four of us, but not every track is done like that: for instance, on the heavy track 'Headlong', I was in the studio for a couple of days to get some things out of my system. I thought that maybe I'd be left with a solo album, maybe with a Queen album, I just didn't know and I came up with 'Headlong' and 'I Can't Live With You' – the guys liked them."
Brian on 'Innuendo' (1991)

The Musical Competition

"Stock, Aitken and Waterman are like second hand car salesmen or something. They're awful!"

Roger (1988)

"We didn't really feel threatened (by punk), because we saw that it was still the same people attracting large crowds, like Genesis, Zeppelin and The Who, and even us, and we knew that the man in the street was still aware that music could have different forms, and that it didn't have to be one thing at a time, which is what I don't like about England.

"Punk took a lot of backward steps, like the idea that it was bad to put on a show because that wasn't musically valid, but the end result was good, as a sort of clearing out system, and it was a good time for people to reassess themselves. I do wish it hadn't eventually destroyed The Sex Pistols – I would have loved to be able to talk to them, although I'm sure they wouldn't have listened at the time, because we were something which punk was reacting against."
Brian

"I first heard it (Vanilla Ice's 'Ice Ice Baby') in the fan club downstairs. I just thought, 'Interesting, but nobody will ever buy it because it's crap.' Turns out I was wrong. Next thing, my son's saying it's big here, 'And what are you going to do about it, Dad?' Actually, Hollywood (Records) are sorting it out because they don't want people pillaging what they've just paid so much money for. We don't want to get involved in litigation with other artists ourselves, that doesn't seem very cool really. Anyway, now I think it's quite a good bit of work in its way."
Brian (1991)

Freddie On Freddie

**"The reason we're successful, darling?
My overall charisma, of course."**

(1972)

"It's stupid to say there is no such thing in boarding schools. All the things they say about them are more or less true. All the bullying and everything else. I've had the odd schoolmaster chasing me. It didn't shock me because somehow boarding schools… you're not confronted by it, you are just slowly aware of it. It's going through life.

"There were times when I was young and green. It's a thing schoolboys go through. I've had my share of schoolboy pranks. I'm not going to elaborate any further."
On brutality and homosexuality at boarding schools (1974)

"Art school teaches you to be more fashion conscious, to be always one step ahead."
(1971)

"I'm a man of extremes. I have a soft side and a hard side with not a lot in between. If the right person finds me I can be very vulnerable, a real baby, which is invariably when I get trodden on. But sometimes I'm hard, and when I'm strong no-one can get to me."

"I'm very emotional. Whereas before, I was given time to make my decisions, now nearly all of us are so highly strung we just snap. We always argue but I think that's a healthy sign because we get to the root of the matter and squeeze the best out. But lately so much is happening, it's escalating so fast that everybody wants to know almost instantly, and I certainly get very temperamental.

"You've got to know where to draw the line. But the public always come first – it's a corny thing to say but I mean it. Lately I've been throwing things around which is very unlike me. I threw a glass at someone the other day. I think I'm going to go mad in a few years' time; I'm going to be one of those insane musicians."
(1974)

"Musicians aren't social rejects any more. If you mean 'Have I got upper class parents who put a lot of money into me? Was I spoilt?' – no. My parents were very strict. I wasn't the only

one, I've got a sister. I was at boarding school for nine years so I didn't see my parents that often. That background helped me a lot because it taught me to fend for myself."
(1974)

"I don't like the way my teeth protrude. I'm going to have them done, but I just haven't had the time. Apart from that… I'm perfect."

"I hate pockets in trousers. By the way, I do not wear a hose. My hose is my own. No coke bottle, nothing stuffed down there."
(1974)

"My nodules are still with me. I have these uncouth callouses growing in my interior (throat). From time to time they harm my vocal

dexterity. At the moment, however, I am winning.

"I'm going easy on the red wine and the tour will be planned around my nodules. Actually, I came very near to having an operation but I didn't like the look of the doctor and I was a bit perturbed about having strange instruments forced down my throat."
(1975)

"I want my privacy, and I feel I've given a lot for it. It's like Greta Garbo isn't it? Virgo, same star sign."

"People are apprehensive when they meet me. They think I'm going to eat them. But underneath it all I'm quite shy."
(1976)

"I like leather. I rather fancy myself as a black panther."
(1977)

"Excess is part of my nature. Dullness is a disease. I really need danger and excitement. I've often been warned to stay away from clubs because they are too dangerous. But I revel in that – I'm never scared of putting myself out on a limb."

"Money may not be able to buy happiness, but it can damn well give it!"

"I've made no effort to become a guitar hero because I can't play the fucking guitar!"

"The Jubilee's quite fun, isn't it? I love the Queen. I'm very patriotic. I love all this pomp, of course I do. I love it. She does outrageous things!"
On Queen Elizabeth II's Silver Jubilee (1977)

"Every person who makes a lot of money has a dream he wants to carry out, and I achieved that dream with this wonderful house. Whenever I watched Hollywood movies set in plush homes with lavish decor, I wanted that for myself, and now I've got it. But to me it was much more important to get the damn thing than to actually go and live in it. Maybe the challenge has worn off now. I'm very much like that – once I get something I'm not that keen on it anymore. I still love the house, but the real enjoyment is that I've achieved it. Sometimes, when I'm alone at night, I imagine that when I'm 50 I'll creep into that house as my refuge, and then I'll start making it a home. Anyway, as it is, I can only spend 60 days a year in England for tax reasons."
(1981)

"I was wearing a white scarf and holding a glass of wine when I was introduced to Prince Andrew. But I was so nervous I didn't realise my scarf was dangling in the drink. There I was trying to be really cool and suddenly the Prince said, 'Freddie, I don't think you really want this getting wet.' He squeezed out the scarf and that broke the ice between us. I said, 'Thank goodness you've put me at ease. Now I can use the odd bit of dirty language.' He really got into the spirit of things and even had a dance. He's really quite hip in those sort of situations. I have a lot of respect for Royalty, I'm a tremendous patriot."
(1981)

"It's not a question of money anymore. I spend money like it's nothing. You know, I could be penniless tomorrow, but I'd get back, somehow."
(1982)

"I can be very soft, very slushy and mushy."
(1983)

"If I tried that on, people would start yawning, 'Oh God, here's Freddie saying he's gay because it's very trendy'."
After 'I Want To Break Free' video (1984)

"I like to ridicule myself. I don't take myself too seriously. I wouldn't wear these clothes if I was serious. The one thing that keeps me going is that I laugh at myself."

"For God's sake, if I want to make big confessions about my sex life, would I go to The Sun, of all papers, to do it? There's no fucking way I'd do that. I'm too intelligent."

"I enjoy being a bitch. I enjoy being surrounded by bitches. Boredom is the biggest disease in the world, darling. Sometimes I think there must be more to life than rushing round the world like a mad thing getting bored."

"I was caught up in being a star and I thought 'This is the way a star behaves'. Now I don't give a damn. I want to do things my way and have fun. If all my money ended tomorrow, I'd still go about like I had lots of money because that's what I used to do before. I'll always walk around like a Persian Poppinjay and no one's gonna stop me.

"I love living life to the full – that's my nature. Nobody tells me what to do."
(1985)

"I would have loved to have been on the Band Aid record, but I only heard about it in Germany. I don't know if they would have had me on the record anyway. I'm a bit old."
(1985)

"I never carry money, just like the real Queen. If I fancy something in a shop I always ask someone on our staff to buy it."

"Darling, I'm simply dripping with money. It may be vulgar but it's wonderful! All I want from life is to make lots of money and spend it."

"When I look back on all that black varnish, chiffon, satin and that, I think God, what was I doing?"

"I'm a big, macho, sexual object and I'm very arrogant. So most people dismiss me because of that. They don't know what I'm really like."

"I can't carry on rocking the way I have done in the past. It is all too much. It's no way for a grown man to behave. I have stopped my nights of wild partying. That's not because I'm ill but down to age. I'm no spring chicken. Now I prefer to spend my time at home. It is part of growing up."

"The album track 'Living On My Own' is very me. I have to go around the world living in hotels. You can have a whole shoal of people you know looking after you, but in the end they all go away.

"But, I'm not complaining. I'm living on my own time and having a boogie time.

"When you're a celebrity, it's hard to approach somebody and say 'Look, I'm normal underneath'. Then what happens is they tread all over me because by trying to be normal to somebody, suddenly I've come out of my shell and become far more vulnerable than most people.

"Because I'm successful and have a lot of money, a lot of greedy people prey on me. But that's something I've learned to deal with.

"I'm riddled with scars and I just don't want anymore."

"I've got a few good friends, a big house and I can go wherever I want whenever I want… but the more money you make the more miserable you get. It just so happens that I have a lot of money."

"I'm a very emotional person, a person of real extremes, and that's often destructive both to myself and others."

"I love everybody, you know. I love all these beautiful brown bodies whoever they are. I think I'm a mother figure to many people. I love to share problems with people."
In Brazil (1985)

The Band On Freddie

"Freddie's just his natural self: just a poof, really."
Roger (1974)

"The first thing I remember about meeting him was that he seemed like a Gypsy. He was nominally living with his parents, but stayed with whoever he wanted. He invited me round to his house where he had this little stereo and played me some Hendrix. I said, 'This guy really makes use of stereo', so we went from one speaker to the other, finding out how he produced those sounds."
Brian

"Freddie always looked like a star and acted like a star even though he was penniless. He was captivated by Hendrix. When he and Roger had their clothes stall in Kensington Market, they shut down for the day when Hendrix died. They were in on the beginnings of what became Glam Rock with that stall, though some of it was incredibly tatty. When we started sharing a flat, Fred would bring home these great bags of stuff, pull out some horrible strip of cloth and say, 'Look at this beautiful garment! This is going to fetch a fortune!'"
Brian (1991)

"We were recording an album next door to The Sex Pistols. One day Sid Vicious stumbled in and yelled at Freddie, ''Ullo Fred, so you've really brought ballet to the masses then?' Freddie just turned round and said, 'Ah, Mr Ferocious. Well, we're trying our best dear!'"
Roger

"Freddie doesn't talk anymore because he's a little tired of Queen and himself being misrepresented. I think anybody who meets Freddie would be in for a bit of a surprise. He's not quite the prima donna you might imagine. Obviously, he's a positive character, but so are we all. When all is said and done he works damned hard and puts on a good show."
Roger (1981)

"Freddie is a dominating character, but we all have a big say in the group. The fact that we share songwriting duties – I came up with 'Radio Ga Ga', for instance – does save one's own integrity."
Roger

Playing Live

"I'd like to be carried on stage by six nubile slaves with palms and all."

Freddie (1974)

"I'd like a couple of weeks off, but you've got to push yourself. But we're at a stage in our careers, my dear, where it's just got to be done. I shall be resting on my laurels soon.

"To put it another way, I shall try and reap my profits. I've worked my ass off these past few months. I've worked till I've dropped and after a while you physically can't do it."
Freddie (1974)

"Yes, it was a heavy tour, but it put us in a different bracket overnight. It's a tour we had to do and I think now we've done it we can do the next British tour on our own terms, exactly how we like.

"With this tour we were booked in well beforehand at semi-big venues and, by the time we came to doing them, we had the album out, we'd got a bit of TV exposure and everything escalated. I think if we'd waited we could have done all the big venues – it's just a matter of timing. But I'm glad we did the tour when we did. Even though there was a lot of physical and mental strain – so many things to worry about other than music."
Freddie (1974)

"I just like people to put their own interpretation on my songs. Really, they are just little fairy stories. Last night (at Sunderland) I felt really evil when I came on stage – when I'm out there I'm really in a world of my own, I go up there and have a good time. It's the audience participation that counts and last night they were really great, I felt I could have gone into the audience and had a rave. Just Freddie Mercury poncing on stage and having a good time."
Freddie (1974)

"The Hyde Park gig was really high. The occasion rather than the gig, you know, the tradition of Hyde Park. I went to see the first one with the Floyd and Jethro Tull – a great atmosphere and the feeling that it was free. We felt that it would be nice to revive that but it was fraught with heartache because there were so many problems. Trying to get the place was hard enough, let alone in the evening. We had to make compromises and in the end, because the schedule overran by half an hour, the loss meant we couldn't do an encore."
Brian (1976)

"We thought it was important to actually visit people again. Unless people see you in their home town, it can almost seem that you don't exist. It's also a big relief to us because, having done the big barns, it's nice to be somewhere where people can actually see and hear you.

"The advantage of what we're doing this time is that, because our sound and light systems are better than ever, we can really knock audiences in the stomach. The only real disadvantage is that not everybody can get to see us – but I think that those who do have a much better time. It's great fun, too, because the response is much more immediate and rewarding.

"In the larger venues you tend to lose that intimacy, but on the other hand you gain something else. You get a feeling of an event, and the more people there are, the greater the tension becomes. As a result it makes you work harder, particularly to reach the people at the back.

"I doubt very much whether we will be going back to large venues in England, because there aren't actually many good ones. Bingley was quite good, but it's dirty and nasty for the people who come to watch. The NEC in Birmingham is the same – and it was definitely far too big.

"It's nice to do those sort of places once and see what they're like, but there aren't many we'd want to go back to. I wouldn't want to do Earls Court again, nor Wembley, and it's quite possible that after doing Alexandra Palace we won't want to do that. But it's worth a try, because we're trying to do some special things with Ally Pally. We wanted to do one big gig in London to sweep up all the people we couldn't otherwise cover.

"We don't like to be artificially exclusive. I'd hate to get to the point where people who genuinely want to see us and who couldn't queue up for the tickets can't see us at all."
Brian (1979)

"We've all got a different opinion on when, where and how a tour should take place. We needed a good year to release this record, and this whole touring idea, if we come to an agreement, will be delayed for a few further months too. We don't want to repeat ourselves whatever happens – if we do decide to go on tour, it'll be from a different angle than our tour three years ago."
Roger (1989)

"Contrary to what people think, you don't tour just to make money or be adulated, or whatever. You need a very positive drive to keep yourself convinced all the time that it's worth doing yourself. So if we didn't think that the music was still getting to new places or doing interesting things, then none of us would feel like doing it."
Brian (1980)

"It's not really the same approach as Kiss, where I would say the show is everything, although it probably doesn't end up looking a whole lot different. Our idea is to get all the impact of the music across in that short time. It's only once a year, and you really have to try and emphasise every note!"
Brian (1980)

"I like people to go away from a Queen show feeling fully entertained, having had a good time. I think Queen songs are pure escapism, like going to see a good film – after that, they can go away and say that was great, and go back to their problems. I don't want to change the world with our music. There are no hidden messages in our songs, except for some of Brian's."
Freddie (1981)

"There are certain people who we rely on getting (on tour), like Trip Khalaf, who's our permanent sound mixer, and James Devenney, our permanent monitor mixer – that's so crucial, and I think one of the most difficult jobs in the world, because it's equally important to have a good sound on stage as to get it good out front, and if either one's lacking you do a bad show."
Brian

"I don't know how those ballet people do it – the same steps every night! I couldn't perform in that framework."
Freddie (1981)

"We do have a lot of power. We just hope we can divert it in the right direction... I know it looks like a Nuremberg Rally, but our fans are sensible people, they're creating the situation as much as we are, it's not that we're leading them like sheep... You just play music which excites people, which interests them. It's rock 'n' roll, there's no philosophical reason why we should be there... Touring is certainly the most immediately fulfilling part of what we do, and it's not really a big strain – mentally or physically – because we're well organised, we know how to do it. All you have to worry about is playing well on the night. For me, it's by far the best part of being in the band. Suddenly life becomes simple again."
Brian (1980)

"We usually set aside around three weeks for rehearsal for an upcoming tour. But the first two weeks of that are usually spent talking, so then there's this great panic when we realise we've only got a week left to get through everything.

"Normally we would spend everything we anticipate making on the staging for the show. It's only when we do places as large as Wembley Stadium that we can actually make some money out of it. With doing it for two nights, we manage to pay our expenses on the first night and show a profit on the second."
Brian (1983)

"I find even when people have let you down, you just want to go on stage. It's very gratifying to know that all sorts of people want you."
Freddie

"I have to win people over, otherwise it's not a successful gig. It's my job to make sure people have a good time. That's part of my duty. It's all to do with feeling in control."
Freddie (1985)

"Four weeks of rehearsals is more than we have ever done in our career. I think we are probably the best live band in the world at the moment and we are going to prove it – no-one who comes to see us will be disappointed."
Roger (1986)

"I like to have a support. It's nice to go on to an audience which is warmed up, and also if it's a good support it gives you something to work off. We had Gary Moore in Germany, who, as you know, is a very good player, and I'd be sat backstage hearing all this going on out front and

thinking, 'Jesus, I've got to go on and follow this guy'. But it gets your adrenalin going and you go out there and play to kill."
Brian

"I badly want to play live – with or without Queen. If we can't come to some kind of arrangement within the band, I'll get my own project together, but I can't stand it much longer. I want to go back on stage as fast as possible!"
Brian (1989)

"I want to change the cycle of album, world tour, album, world tour. Maybe we will tour, but it will be for totally different reasons. I've personally had it with these bombastic lights and staging effects. I don't think a 42-year-old man should be running around in his leotard any more."
Freddie (1989)

"The demand for us to tour is getting to be a pain in the ass."
Roger (1989)

"We'd like to tour in a different way. Visually all the tours are very similar. We'd like to step out of the standard hard rock light show."
Roger (1989)

"Well, actually, we're at something of a crossroads at the moment. We're still very much alive in the studio – perhaps more so now than ever before – but this will be the first time we've released an album without promoting it with a tour. You see, at the moment Freddie just doesn't want to tour. He doesn't feel that he can, so the touring part of my life has come to a complete stop. It's a terrible shame because Roger, John and myself all love playing live and feel that part of the reason for making an album is to be able to take it out on the road and have fun. So, taking the touring side of things away messed up my life really – without exaggeration. I feel it's taken the whole balance out of my life. If he doesn't enjoy it or feel happy with it then I guess you can't do anything about it. But it's hard for us to deal with because the rest of us would still really love to play live."
Brian (1990)

"When you come off stage there's so much adrenalin flowing and so much going on in your head that we find we have to go out somewhere and be noisy for a while and come down gradually. When you're on stage there's such a communication thing going on with the audience – you feel so close and you're reaching out and it's so emotional – that when you come off stage there's a terrible void, an empty feeling, and all you want to do is get close to lots of people again."
Brian (1990)

Live Aid

**"The rest of us played okay, but Freddie was out there and took it to
another level. It wasn't just Queen fans – he connected with everyone."**
Brian (1985)

"I'm so powerful on stage that I seem to have created a monster. When I'm performing I'm an extrovert, yet inside I'm a completely different man."
Freddie (1985)

"We didn't know Bob Geldof at all. When 'Do They Know It's Christmas' was out, that was a lot of the newer acts. For the gig, he wanted to get a lot of the established acts. Our first reaction was, we didn't know – 20 minutes, no soundcheck!

"When it became apparent that it was going to happen, we'd just finished touring Japan and ended up having a meal in the hotel discussing whether we should do it… and we said yes.

"It was the one day that I was proud to be involved in the music business. A lot of days you certainly don't feel that! But the day was fabulous, people forgot that element of competitiveness… it was a good morale-booster for us too, because it showed us the strength of support we had in England, and it showed us what we had to offer as a band."
John (1985)

"We've always had our quiet periods and comebacks. I think Live Aid proved we didn't need backdrops or cover of darkness. Geldof called Live Aid a jukebox, so it seemed obvious to us to simply play the hits and get off."
Brian (1985)

"We don't do enough shows these days, and I'd like to do more. I'll remember Live Aid till the day I die."
Brian (1989)

Playing Technique

"I had this idea... I wanted the sound to sing and have that thickness but yet still have an edge so that it could articulate. So my dad and I designed the guitar... the one that was made from an old fireplace."

Brian

"My father taught me to play ukulele-banjo in the style of George Formby – it's a pretty good instrument that's tuned the same way as a ukulele, but has the same sort of sound vellum as a banjo, and from the chords I learnt on that, I taught myself the guitar."

"My first guitar was a very cheap acoustic Spanish type guitar with steel strings, and was much too big for me when I got it. I can remember being dwarfed by this thing, getting it in bed on my birthday morning, and I thought it was very shiny and new and exciting. Later, I put a pick-up on it, which my father and I made out of some button magnets with a coil wound round – it worked as well! We plugged it into a radio, into the auxiliary input, and it sounded pretty good, with a very sharp, penetrating clear sound, which I can't really get now.

"I found it quite easy to pick up playing guitar – I was taking piano lessons at the time, which I never really enjoyed, because it was a chore to do the requisite half hour piano practice, and I always ended up banging the piano and swearing and walking away in disgust, whereas I always went to the guitar for pleasure, which is why, I suppose, my guitar playing progressed faster."
Brian (1983)

"I had this idea… I wanted the sound to sing and have that thickness but yet still have an edge so that it could articulate. So my dad and I designed the guitar… the one that was made from an old fireplace.

"My personal opinion is that you can theorise all you like, but if you hit on something that sounds good, then stick with it. I don't believe in getting too technical. If it works and sounds good – then that's it for me.

"I like a big neck – thick, flat and wide. I lacquered the fingerboard with Rustin's Plastic Coating. The tremolo is interesting in that the arm's made from an old bicycle saddle bag carrier, the knob at the end's off a knitting needle and the springs are valve springs from an old motorbike."
Brian

"I use coins instead of a plectrum because they're not flexible. I think you get more control if all the flexing is due to the movement in your fingers. You get better contact with the strings, and depending on how tightly you hold it, you have total control over how hard it's being played, and because of its round surface and the serration, by turning it different ways you can get different sounds, like a fairly soft sound, or a slightly grating sound on the beginning of the note which actually lends a bit of distinction to the notes, especially when you're using the guitar at high volume, as I generally do."
Brian

"I don't think my playing has progressed that much technically in terms of pure playing, and I could play almost everything I can play now when I was about sixteen. I sometimes think that's a bad thing, but I see it in lots of other people as well: Jeff Beck and Eric Clapton. You fairly quickly reach a stage when you're practising very intensely and where you can express most of what you want to play, and after that, I think, you become better as an all-round musician and your taste improves, but I don't think your technical ability gets much better and you reach a plateau."
Brian

"Basically, I'm a real rock guitarist, but the term 'rock' is really wide these days. I like nearly everything that sounds honest and has some kind of statement. My favourite guitarists at the moment are Jeff Beck and Eric Clapton, although I like Yngwie Malmsteen as well. I get great enjoyment jamming with people like that, and seeing as Queen hardly tour these days I get quite a few opportunities to do so."
Brian (1989)

"When Hendrix came along, it just seemed to be such a great opening of doors – he seemed to push it along so fast in such a short time. As a guitarist, I've a reluctance to admit another guitarist's as good as he is but there's still nobody who can approach him for inventiveness, pure sound and style and everything.

"I find that a lot of people who used to impress me are the ones who still do – like Jeff Beck, Clapton… and Tony Iommi from Black Sabbath is a great player, and very much underrated. I like the guitarists in Def Leppard too.

"The kids coming up now (who) take someone like Eddie Van Halen, for instance, as a starting point, are going to go a long way. I mean, there was no-one around like that when we were starting out."
Brian (1990)

World Champions

**"They wouldn't let us into Russia.
They thought we'd corrupt the youth or something."**
Freddie (1986)

"We tour for our own satisfaction and also to increase the status of the group. It's a long-term thing rather than a short-term tour. The important thing is that we're not in it for any short-term benefits. If we break big we'll be all right in the end. It's all or nothing.

"We seem to be cracking it here but England's not really the be-all-and-end-all because you can do a tour with a lot of equipment and you don't make a lot of money. Even with the copies of the album we sell in England we might only break even. The new one cost £25,000 to make."
John (1974)

"We haven't been to America yet, but the first album did quite well there. Apparently we're known to an extent on the east coast, and in the south."
Roger (1974)

"We did what we had to do, anyway. Sure, a whole tour would have helped us a bit more, but there's no such thing as 'We lost our chance'. I still believe that the time is right for us there and we're going back pretty soon. We really did it – 'cause when we came back you should have seen the write-ups. They were beautiful and they just want us to come back as soon as we can. They are just waiting on new product."
Freddie, on quitting a US tour half-way through (1974)

"We got a lot of FM radio play (in America), and a lot of backing for that first album from people who played four or five tracks of it to death, and that gave us a really good grounding in America. We didn't tour in America, which was a shame, but we were just too busy doing other things at the time. It's very much to the credit of Jack Nelson, who was brought in from America to manage us on Trident's behalf, and knew the American scene, that we toured there immediately after making our second album, supporting Mott The Hoople; that was really one of the best things we ever did."
Brian

"I liked it there, the lifestyle, the art – I'd go back there tomorrow if I could."
Freddie on Japan (1975)

"We're riding on the crest of a wave and things are opening up for us here."
Freddie on a New York gig (1976)

"I don't know about this anymore. Here I am, just a bloody rock'n'roll drummer and all these thousands of kids are going crackers. It doesn't seem right somehow, with Britain in a recession."
Roger on South America (1981)

"We really were nervous. We had no right to automatically expect the works from an alien territory. I don't think they'd ever seen such an ambitious show, with this lighting and effects."
Freddie on South America (1981)

"As long as we feel a sense of achievement and that we are breaking new ground, like doing the South American tours, and planning something like the Far East, we're happy, and we ought to continue."
Freddie (1981)

"In a way I was surprised that we didn't get more criticism for playing South America. I didn't think we were being used as tools by political régimes, although obviously you have to co-operate with them. We were playing for the people. We didn't go there with the wool pulled over our eyes. We fully know what the situation is like in some of those countries, but for a time we made thousands of people happy. Surely that must count for something. We weren't playing for the government, we were playing to lots of ordinary Argentinian people. In fact, we were asked to meet the President, President Viola, and I refused. Didn't want to meet him, because that would have been playing into their hands. We went there to do some rock music for the people. I wouldn't mind playing Russia at some time. But over there you have to be carefully vetted by the government. The Russian authorities like Cliff Richard and Elton John, but Queen are still considered a little bit wild."
Roger (1981)

"In Argentina we were Number One when that stupid war was going on and we had a fantastic time there, and that can only be good. Music is totally international."
Roger (1982)

"It's our young men killing their young men. There's no glory in being blown to bits."
Freddie on the Falklands War (1982)

"It's wonderful. The sunshine makes such a difference. People are really allowed to flower here. They're a wonderful audience and I love their displays of emotion. They get over-excited sometimes, but I can bring the whip down and show them who's in control."
Freddie, Brazil, 1985

"I don't know why they get so excited about me dressing up as a woman. There are loads of transvestites here. Just go and look on any street corner and you'll find them."
Freddie, Brazil, 1985

"Well, there was a bit of trouble, a fight between some of the crowd and a cameraman, but? I don't go on dressed like that to provoke them you know. Still, it's a good story so what the fuck?"
Freddie on Brazilian crowd reaction to his drag sequence (1986)

"It's a tremendous market. If you crack it here the amount of money you make is tremendous. We've opened South America to the rest of the world. We came to South America originally because we were invited down: they wanted four wholesome lads to play nice music. Now I'd like to buy up the entire continent and install myself as president."
Freddie, Brazil (1985)

"South America? The problem over there is that they're corrupt; life is cheap."
Freddie (1986)

"South America was a completely new thing for Queen. I'd like to play there again, especially with 300,000 people singing along to your songs.

That was an energy you can't ignore. In principle it's secondary where you play, because fans react in a similar way all over the world. I just want to play live again – and Europe would be just as good as the Eastern bloc or South America."
Brian (1989)

"There's lots of money to be made."
Freddie on playing Sun City

"Throughout our career we've been a very non-political group. We enjoy going to new places. We've toured America and Europe so many times that it's nice to go somewhere different. Everybody's been to South Africa, it's not as if we're setting a precedent. Elton John's been there. Rod Stewart, Cliff Richard. I know there can be a bit of a fuss, but apparently we're very popular down there. Basically, we want to play wherever the fans want to see us."
John on playing Sun City

"We're totally against apartheid and all it stands for, but I feel we did a lot of bridge building. We actually met musicians of both colours. They all welcomed us with open arms. The only criticism we got was from outside South Africa."
Brian on playing Sun City

"In a way I do regret playing. In some ways I would defend what we did. I mean basically we play music to people – lots of them, preferably – and I think a lot of crap is talked over here about things people don't really know about."
Roger on playing Sun City

"The Russians still think we're very decadent. We want to play China as well, and Korea. John and I spent a holiday in Korea, and it's a fascinating place."
Roger

"I think our whole image became too diffused for America. They hated what they felt were gay overtones of 'I Want To Break Free', the drag stuff. Americans found that very distasteful, whereas everyone else thought it was a laugh."
Brian (1989)

The Image

**"The concept of Queen is to be regal and majestic.
Glamour is part of us, and we want to be dandy."**

Freddie

"When I look back on all that black nail varnish and stuff I think, 'God, what did I do?' I used to feel a need for all that on stage. It made me feel more secure. But now I don't… I've grown up a bit."
Roger (1974)

"We've had the name for years now, believe it or not – most people don't – and it was Freddie's idea. It was just a reflection of the social world we were in at the time when he and I were working together in Kensington Market – it was good then. In those days there was a pretty eccentric crowd there, people in sombreros and a lot of them were gay and a lot of them pretended to be, and it just seemed to fit in. I didn't like the name originally and neither did Brian, but we got used to it. We thought that once we'd get established the music would become the identity more than the name."
Roger (1974)

"We're not really choreographed. It's just that Freddie is the natural extrovert and I suppose I'm a foil to that."
Brian (1974)

"The agony we went through to have those ('Sheer Heart Attack' cover) pictures taken. Can you imagine trying to convince the others to

cover themselves in Vaseline and then have a hose of water turned on them?

"The end result is four members of the band looking decidedly unregal, tanned and healthy, and as drenched as if they've been sweating for a week.

"Everyone was expecting some sort of cover. A 'Queen III' cover, really, but this is completely new. It's not that we're changing altogether - it's just a phase we are going through.

"We're still as poncy as ever. We're still the dandies we started out to be. We're just showing people we're not merely a load of poofs, that we are capable of other things."
Freddie (1974)

"I think I strike a lot of people as being shy and introverted. But a lot of people are the biggest big heads in the world underneath that exterior."
Brian (1975)

"When I started off, rock bands were all wearing jeans – and suddenly here's Freddie Mercury in a Zandra Rhodes frock with make-up and black nail varnish. It was totally outrageous."
Freddie

"I used to think that there were people, a breed of person, who was a 'star'. But the more I've met people who I thought were 'natural', the more I realise that everyone puts on an act to some extent. Nobody can be exactly natural on stage."
Brian (1980)

"I thought up the name Queen… It's just a name, but it's very regal obviously, and it sounds splendid. It's a strong name, very universal and immediate. It had a lot of visual potential and was open to all sorts of interpretations. I was certainly aware of the gay connotations, but that was just one facet of it."
Freddie

"It seems to be a matter of timing. For instance, the other night I saw a band, Warrant, that dresses the way we were dressing 15 years ago. Last year there were a lot of bands like Led Zeppelin, so maybe it's our turn."
Roger (1989)

The Media

"I don't pretend to understand the workings of the journalistic mind."

Roger (1974)

"I think, to an extent, we're a sitting target because we've gained popularity quicker than most bands and we've been talked about more than any other band in the last month, so it's inevitable. Briefly, I'd be the first one to respect fair criticism. I think it would be wrong if all we got were good reviews – but it's when you get unfair, dishonest reviews where people haven't done their homework that I get annoyed."
Freddie (1974)

"There are really only two things that hurt: firstly, we're called a hype – that's one thing we're not. We're making it in the old-fashioned way, which is initially through selling records, through playing concerts, enabling the record company to get behind you for the second album. The other thing is that they cast doubts on your musicianship, which is one thing we're really sure about. Obviously we think we're bloody good. Oh yes, and we've been accused of being a part of supermarket rock – which is a bit rich when you write your own material."
Roger (1974)

"We were just totally ignored for so long, then completely slagged off and slated by everyone. In a way that was a good start for us. There's no kind of abuse that wasn't thrown at us. It was only around the time of 'Sheer Heart Attack' that it began to change. I'm always affected by criticism. I think most artists are even if they say they're not. It doesn't matter how far you get, if someone says you're a load of shit it hurts. But that was just a press response, because for the rest it was always building up very steadily."
Brian (1977)

"Fred's been bitten worse than most because he's up there at the front, so he tends to get most of the stick. I've always talked to people whenever possible, but I've been taken for a ride many times. In the end, we found it was easiest for us not to talk to people, and that's why there have been no interviews for quite a while.

"These days I get more angry about the way other people are treated, rather than us. I've come to terms with our relationship with the press – basically they just don't like what we stand for. They say that we've gone commercial, but the truth is we simply sell more records now. Nothing's changed in the way that we write."
Brian (1979)

"I don't think that any critic can be more critical of us than we are anyway. If we're coming up with ideas, then one of us will be so cutting and caustic about it while it's being done that nothing much gets past if it's in any way suspect. By the time it gets to the public, it's been through all that."
Brian (1980)

"There are lots of little mechanisms built into the relationship between a musician and the press, which means – almost inevitably – that you fall out. But it happened very early to us, so perhaps it doesn't apply. Generally, I could write the reviews of our albums, the good ones and the bad ones. It's a very limited view of what goes on, as soon as something becomes successful, it can't be worth anything... I did think in the beginning it was important to keep the lines of communication open, to talk to everybody. In the end though, after many experiences, you find that it really doesn't come out. If the guy has stated already that he hates you, and can't see anything in you that is

worthwhile, then nine times out of ten, if you spend your time trying to convince him how good you are, he goes away and writes what he thought anyway! We do have a reputation for not wanting to talk to people, which is really not that true most of the time, if we have time we'll always talk. But if somebody slags you off in a way you don't think is fair, you don't want to talk to them again."
Brian (1980)

"We had never really got on with the press and had a lot of enemies there, but by that time, just about everyone in the press was against us, and quite blatantly so. So our silence wasn't through choice, it was really having no-one to talk to who was going to write anything which would be of any use to us, so we thought it best not to bother, although reluctantly, particularly in my case, because I like talking to people and I think there's always something to gain from it. I know it happens to everybody else as well, and it's a normal consequence of success in England - a lot of people resent your success, and a lot of people also resented Fred's demeanour on stage, interpreting it as a sort of arrogance in his private life, which he doesn't have. He's a performer first, and off stage he's pretty shy on the whole."
Brian (1983)

"The thing is I believe in personalities not papers. I'm not interested in us versus the New Musical Express. People do think that because I don't do interviews I've got this thing against the press. And it's not true."
Freddie (1986)

"I don't like doing interviews because if you plonk a tape recorder in front of me I just clam up, you know?"
Freddie (1986)

"We've all been hauled through the tabloids now. It's very strange that we've been moderately famous for some time but not tabloid fodder until the last three years. It's not been pleasant. Some papers want a certain kind of news, and it can wreck people's lives and I don't think they have any sense of responsibility about it."
Brian (1989)

"We don't do many interviews because they get to be really boring after a while. Sometimes they're quite interesting though, because you get direct reactions to the LPs. And it gives us the opportunity to support our record company with their promotion, and that's only fair. It starts getting tedious when we do one interview after the other, and everyone asks the same questions."
Brian (1989)

"Even when the albums were selling a lot, the critics generally trashed them. You thought, 'I wonder what the truth is? Are we any good or not? Where's the yardstick?' You never know, so you can only believe in yourself."
Brian (1991)

"Criticism used to hurt me when I thought it could affect our careers. Nowadays it's all irrelevant. We know the opinions of the people that matter to us, and critics don't fall under that heading."
Brian

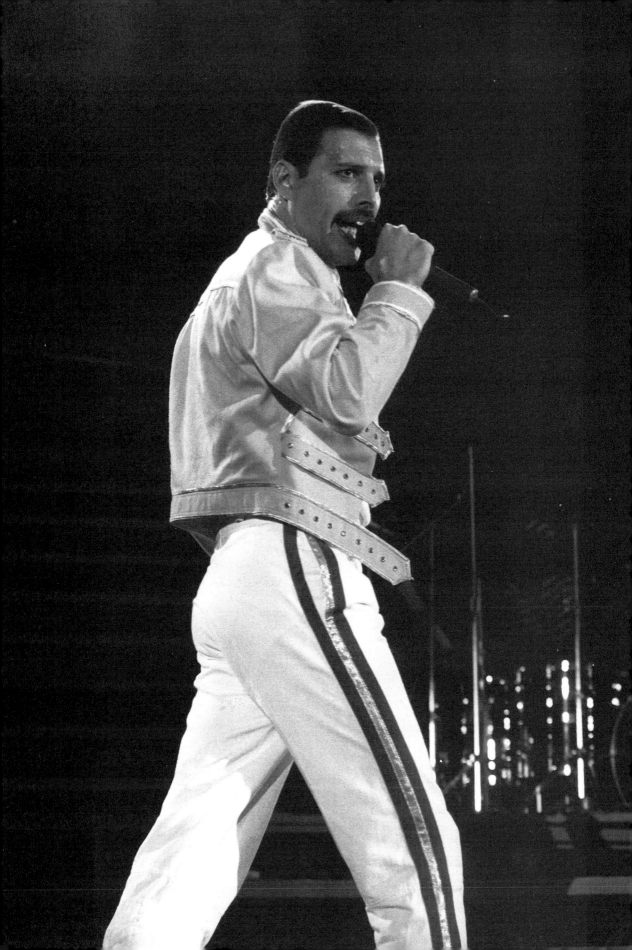

The Music Business

"After three albums, people thought we were driving around in Rolls-Royces already."

Brian

"The moment we made a demo we were aware of the sharks. We had such amazing offers from people saying, 'We'll make you the next T Rex', but we were very, very careful not to jump straight in. Literally, we went to about every company before we finally settled. We didn't want to be treated like an ordinary band."
Freddie (1974)

"After three albums, people thought we were driving around in Rolls-Royces already. Actually we were deeply in debt and our accountants explained to us that the management contract was set up so that most of the money would never get through to us. That's when we started to feel very resentful. The debts were a terrible pressure. We couldn't pay lighting companies, sound companies. It affected our private lives too. John had a baby by then and he was still living in a bedsit because Trident refused to give him a couple of thousand for a deposit on a house."
Brian

"As far as Queen are concerned our old management is deceased. They cease to exist in any capacity with us whatsoever. One leaves them behind like one leaves excreta. We feel so relieved!"
Freddie (1974)

"After the first LP, Trident had to go around all the record companies again to see what offers they could get for us, but unfortunately, they were selling us as part of a package of their production (company), which included Eugene Wallace and Mark Ashton, and they wanted the package accepted as a whole. But suddenly, there was a move from EMI – Roy Featherstone sent us a telegram which asked us not to sign with anyone else until we'd talked to him: he was very keen and he got us, and I think, in the end, he did sign the whole package of Mark Ashton and everything. But it had taken an awfully long time, partially because Trident had to do all the negotiations, as our hands were tied, and we actually put on the sleeve of the album that this was the result of three years' work, because we were upset and felt that the

record was old-fashioned by the time it came out. Lots of stuff had happened in the meantime particularly David Bowie and Roxy Music, who were our sort of generation, but who had already made it, and we felt that it would look like we were jumping on their bandwagon, whereas we'd actually had all that stuff in the can from a very long time before, and it was extremely frustrating."
Brian

"At one point, two or three years after we began, we nearly disbanded. We felt it wasn't working, there were too many sharks in the business and it was all getting too much for us. But something inside us kept us going and we learned from our experiences, good and bad. We didn't make any money until the fourth album, 'Night At The

Opera'. Most of our income was consumed by litigation and things like that."
Freddie (1975)

"It (the split with Trident) brought on things I never realised. Trust became a very funny word – you just had to keep your defences up."
Freddie (1977)

"It's still a big problem organising everything, but we're very lucky in having some great people working for us. We can go anywhere and know that when we walk on stage for the sound check, it'll all be working, which is a wonderful feeling of security. We also have other people working for us in different capacities, because we now manage ourselves and in the end everybody leaves the decision to us. It's not a big operation – people tend to think of the vast Queen machine swinging into action, but we only have four or five people actually working for us, and we pick up the rest when we go on tour.

"We went round and talked in person to a few managers… but John Reid seemed to be the only one we could all agree about – we liked his approach and the style of his operation. We later bought ourselves out of John Reid as well, but it was more out of a feeling that nothing was happening any more – it wasn't so much a

conflict as a feeling that we weren't getting any further in the relationship, and the creative management thing wasn't there as much as it had been at the start. We obviously owe some of our success to both Trident and to John – Trident got us making records and hits, for instance – but the whole John Reid time was a period when we made very big strides."
Brian

"We think it's far better to deal with things ourselves. We still have people working for us, but in the end everything comes back to the band. At times there have been difficulties and there's been a strain because you can get a polarisation within the group in any situation where there is a choice of what to do. In fact, I think we were in real danger of splitting up when the John Reid situation was getting sticky."
Brian (1979)

"We liked the Mountain Studios, in Switzerland, and the location very much, and after making 'Jazz' we said, as a joke, 'Do you want to sell it?' The lady who runs the place told us that the owners were, in fact, thinking of selling it, because it was making a loss. We finally met the guys who owned it – it was partly Swiss and partly Dutch owned – who weren't really

interested in the recording side and just had it as an investment, which wasn't making money for them. We sat down and came to the conclusion that it wasn't making money because they weren't committed enough to running it as a studio which serves people's needs. So we made them an offer, and eventually we got it.

"What we're trying to do is improve it in as many ways as we can. The first thing we did was to lower the prices – because it was expensive, which I think put it out of reach of people in England, especially as Switzerland is such an expensive place to live anyway. We've arranged an accommodation system whereby if people go out there we can put them up in old-style Swiss chalets. It's great – you can have a really good time there. I shall unashamedly plug it!"
Brian (1979)

"We didn't particularly want the job (of managing ourselves), but we decided it was the best way of getting precisely what we wanted and controlling our own destiny."
Brian (1982).

"We were getting too close to each other… getting on each other's nerves which happens periodically. This time we said: 'Let's take a break and give ourselves some breathing space. Let's do individual things, then we can come back to Queen when we actually feel motivated.' We took about five months off work, up until August this year. During this time we met and talked a lot, but we didn't actually do anything. We wanted the next album we made to be in a new situation. We were trying to break from our old record company in America, which was important. We didn't want to deliver another album in that situation.

"There was that feeling that we might just be making another Queen album and putting it back into the machine. We didn't want that, and it's all worked out very well. We agreed on Capitol, and signed a deal with them. Suddenly we have a company in America that's really excited to be getting their first Queen album."
Brian (1983)

Fame
(And Its Price)

**"We don't get letters from gay people or anything,
though I've had letters from people saying I look very evil."**
Freddie (1974)

"We aimed for the top slot: we were not going to be satisfied with anything less."
Freddie

"The responsibility now lies with us. But I've always thought of us as a top group. Sounds very big-headed, I know, but that's the way it is. The opportunity of playing with Mott was great but I knew damn well the moment we finished that tour, as far as Britain was concerned we'd be headlining."
Freddie Mercury (1974)

"It's rubbish to say we were hyped. We started playing the really small gigs and then we released an album. There was no big splash of publicity or anything. Now Cockney Rebel – their publicity came before they'd done anything."
Roger (1974)

"I don't care what they say, really. I think people have said things about us and then changed their minds after listening to the album."
Freddie (1974)

"I remember going to Los Angeles the first time, we were sold out a couple of nights in a small place, and I went to see Led Zeppelin at the Forum. And I thought 'Jesus Christ, if we can ever play here, that would be the ultimate dream come true!'"
Brian (1975)

"We're basically very big-headed people, in a sense that we're convinced of what we're doing. If somebody tells us it's rubbish, then our attitude is that the person's misguided rather than we are rubbish."
Brian (1975)

"We've found – without at first realising it – that when people regard you as a successful group, they get afraid to say things. Eventually you find that everyone around you is telling you what you want to hear."
Brian (1979)

"The higher up the ladder you go, the more vicious you have to be to stop yourself falling off."
Freddie

"That was a big thing for us. Suddenly we were stars – we'd had some success in England and America, but we hadn't had adulation and been adored, and suddenly, in Japan, we were pop stars in the same way as The Beatles or The Bay City Rollers, with people screaming at us, which was a big novelty, and we loved it and had a great time.
"The only drawback was that we were a sort of teenybop attraction, but it was some years ago, and when we go back to Japan now, we're lucky enough to have made a smooth transition to having a pretty normal rock audience in Japan of older people of both sexes rather than just the little girls screaming. But it was an inspirational experience, and I think it brought out the acting ability in us, and made us a bit more extrovert on stage."
Brian

"In Japan something clicked. When we went through customs into the airport lounge in Tokyo, there were 3,000 little girls screaming at us. Suddenly we were The Beatles. We literally had to be carried over the heads of these kids. I was half-scared and half-amused. This wasn't a rock band thing, this was being a teen idol. But we had to admit it was fun!"
Brian (1991)

"You're progressing when you get to play Madison Square Garden for one night, then two, then three. You're reaching more people each time, and it's a recognition that the people who enjoyed themselves the first time have come back and brought their friends. It's a good feeling to build all the time. It doesn't mean that in some ways you're not conscious, it's not an artificial aim, getting bigger is not the be-all and end-all. Often if you sell more records, it doesn't mean that the quality of the record is any better."
Brian (1980)

"We just don't want to be seen to fail. That's what keeps us going."
Roger (1982)

"Doing this job is just like being a housewife. Every day I get up and I've got lots of chores to do. Really, you know, it's not very spectacular."
Freddie (1985)

"Half the people think you're gods, and the other half think you're rubbish – there are all these different reactions to you, which if you took seriously you'd go crazy! I think the fact I distanced myself in those years from everything that was happening was a real help. Perhaps I was too insular, waiting for that plateau that never came. Everything changes, and I still don't find changes easy to cope with, even after all these years."
Brian (1989)

"Success has brought me millions and world fame but not the thing we all need – a loving relationship."
Freddie

"I suppose my dad only came to terms with me being a rock musician when he saw us play Madison Square Garden. Until then it was, 'That's OK, but you'll have to get a proper job later.'

"The funny thing is I think I still suffer from the same delusion myself. Sometimes I have problems in dealing with what I am. Right through to playing stadiums, I'd think 'Well you're doing all right for now, but maybe something else will turn up.' Then, when we gave up touring I suddenly realised, 'Oh, you've never really stopped to enjoy this and now it's ending.' That was the beginning of a major crisis for me. My dad died at the same time and my marriage broke up, so for a while I didn't exist as a person."
Brian (1991)

Regal Relationships

**"Our love affair (with Mary Austin) ended in tears,
but a deep bond grew out of it, and that's something nobody
can take away from us. It's unreachable."**
Freddie

"All my lovers asked me why they couldn't replace Mary (Austin) but it's simply impossible. The only friend I've got is Mary and I don't want anybody else. To me, she was my common-law wife. To me, it was a marriage. We believe in each other, that's enough for me. I couldn't fall in love with a man the same way as I have with Mary."
Freddie

"Barbara (Valentin, a German actress) and I have formed a bond that is stronger than anything I've had with a lover for the past six years. To really talk to her and be myself in a way that's very rare."
Freddie (1985)

"I'm just an old slag who gets up every morning, scratches his head and wonders who he wants to fuck."
Freddie (1985)

"Love is Russian roulette for me. No one loves the real me inside, they're all in love with my fame, my stardom?"
Freddie

"I can be a good lover, but I think after all these years I'm not a very good partner for anybody. Maybe my love is dangerous, but who wants their love to be safe?

"I'm possessed by love – isn't everybody? Most of my songs are love ballads and things to do with sadness and torture and pain. I seem to write a lot of sad songs because I'm a very tragic person. But there is always an element of humour at the end.

"In terms of love, you're not in control and I hate that feeling."
Freddie (1985)

"I've had more lovers than Liz Taylor – both male and female – but my affairs never seem to last. I seem to eat people up and destroy them."
Freddie

"It was such an obvious thing for them to say that we expected it. We heard rumours ages ago that they were looking for something and were going to do a piece on it. There was this guy sneaking about Los Angeles for a whole week when we were there and he would ring up my number in the house and say 'It's Anita's brother – I urgently need her' – She doesn't even have a brother!"
Brian (1987) on rumours of his affair with Anita Dobson

"I thought it'd never happen to me. I thought I was a very stable person and not open to anything like that. But life changes, y'know. I kicked and screamed against it, but in the end you do change. You grow, the people you're with grow and sometimes you don't grow together. It actually screwed me up completely. For nearly a year… it wasn't all because of the press but they don't help. Most of it they made up anyway, but there's no point denying it because you just make it worse."
Brian (1989)

"I lived for sex. Amazingly, I've just gone completely the other way. Aids changed my life. I have stopped going out, I've become almost a nun. I was extremely promiscuous, but I've stopped all that. What's more, I don't miss that kind of life.

"Anyone who has been promiscuous should have a (Aids) test. I'm fine. I'm clear."
Freddie (1987)

"My parents are in my will, and so are my cats, but the vast bulk of it will go to Mary. If I dropped dead tomorrow, Mary's the one person I know who could cope with my vast wealth."
Freddie

The Band

**"We'll be the Cecil B De Mille of rock!
Always wanting to do things bigger and better."**

Freddie Mercury, 1971

"Sparks thought that because I was ill, Queen was breaking up, which wasn't really happening, although things were obviously a bit shaky at the time. I got on very well with Ron and Russell Mael, and I still see them occasionally, but despite the fact that I quite like their music, I didn't feel it would be quite right to join them. I also felt a loyalty to Queen and thought that we'd get our strength back in the end."
Brian

"Brian was approached by Sparks who said they would like him to join them as guitarist. But we all treat that sort of thing as everyday and mundane. We're so involved in what we do – anyway we've all had offers to join other bands. We don't give it a second thought.

"But while, say, Roger and I would tell them to piss off, Brian takes his time about being nice to people so they sometimes get the wrong idea. Brian is really too much of a gentleman, which I am not – I am the old tart – but not for one moment did he consider leaving us."
Freddie

"There will come a time when I can't run around on stage because it can look ridiculous, but none of us has any intention of leaving. It would be cowardice to stop now. The chemistry has worked for us, so why kill the goose that lays the golden egg?"
Freddie

"I just like to think that we've come through rock'n'roll, call it what you like, and there are no barriers; it's open. Especially now when everybody's putting their feelers out and they want to infiltrate new territories. This is what I've been trying to do for years. Nobody incorporated ballet. I mean, it sounds so outrageous and so extreme, but I know there's going to come a time when it's commonplace. The term rock'n'roll is just a label one starts off with. I should like to think of it as a vast open door. We just carry on doing as many things as we can in different fields. Labels are confusing, they bounce off me. People want art. They want showbiz. They want to see you rush off in your

limousine. If everything you read in the press about me was true, I would have burnt myself out by now. We will stick to our guns, and if we're worth anything we will live on."
Freddie (1977)

"The best vehicle for each of us is the group. We gain far more by sticking together than by breaking away. Perhaps we'd gain freedom that way, but we'd be losing the vehicle at the same time. We have an equilibrium and we know each other very well. We can normally predict what each other will say in most situations, but we also know there are certain grounds not to be trodden on. So we keep out of each other's private lives, because we're all different. Certainly, at the moment, there's no strain in the band whatsoever.

"I'm extremely happy to be doing what I'm doing at present. It feels more or less the same as it did when we first did it. And I'm sure that Queen will last as long as we feel that it's doing something worthwhile."
Brian (1979)

"I used to think we'd go on for five years, but it's got to the point where we're all actually too old to break up. Can you imagine forming a new band at 40? Be a bit silly, wouldn't it?"
Freddie (1983)

"We've had ups and downs. People think Queen can't do anything wrong. People think we can just stick out an album and it's easy for us. But really it's not. There are varying degrees of success, and we are always conscious that our next album may be our last. We don't like to repeat ourselves, so there is always the chance that people will hate what we do. It's funny, everyone thought Queen had this big master plan to conquer the world, but really we were so excited just to make an album – that was the ambition in itself. None of us knew what was ahead."
Brian (1983)

"After touring America, Europe and Japan we were totally knackered, so we thought we deserved a bit of a rest… It also had a lot to do

with the last album not doing as well as previous LPs. We realised that it hadn't been what a lot of fans wanted or expected from us, so we thought a break would give us the opportunity to think things through a bit."
Roger (1983)

"We did hate each other for a while. Recording 'Jazz' (1978) and those albums we did in Munich – 'The Game' (1980) and 'The Works' (1984) – we got very angry with each other. I left the group a couple of times – just for the day, you know. I'm off and I'm not coming back! We've all done that. You end up quibbling over one note.

"And we always rowed about money. A lot of terrible injustices take place over songwriting. The major one is B-sides. Like, 'Bohemian Rhapsody' sells a million and Roger gets the same writing royalties as Freddie because he did (the B-side) 'I'm In Love With My Car'. There was contention about that for years."
Brian

"I think change is part of it (Queen's success), but constancy of members is the biggest thing… it helps because we know how to work with each other, and also people identify with the four of us as a group, and know what we look like and who we are. It's also important not to have constancy of material… there should be some style to it and maybe there should be some trademarks which crop up, but you should keep exploring new avenues, or else you die of boredom.

"I don't really have the time (for a solo album), and I don't think the time's really right for me yet. I have a lot of ideas stored away in

"There's an inward jealousy all the way through our history. Roger, Brian, John and I all write separately and battle to get as many of our own songs as possible on each album. There's a push, a hunger, a constant fight which is very healthy. In the end, we slug it out."
Freddie

"Putting people like us in a studio is like throwing a bomb. It would just explode. When we're drunk and we've had too much wine, one of us invariably says, 'Come on, let's do it.' However, next day when we've all sobered up, our friendship goes out the window. Suddenly, it's, 'No way am I singing with HIM'."
Freddie

"We still have the rock'n'roll Gypsy mentality. Even after 12 years without a line-up change we still really enjoy the buzz from playing live and the fact that we have hit singles. Some bands in our position might take it all in their stride, but we're still like kids, we get very excited."
Roger (1984)

"We didn't want to split up because we felt that's a mistake so many people have made from The Beatles onwards. It would have been so good if they could have held together for longer. No matter how talented the individuals are, the group is always something more than its components. And we think Queen is an example of a proper group. With all its shortcomings, I think it's worth keeping together. After all the fights we still tend to come up with things that have been through the sieve and are worthwhile… because of all the fighting. We still care."
Brian

boxes, but I don't really want to do it at the moment, because there's enough to do with Queen and my private life."
Brian

"I won't be touring on my own or splitting with Queen. Without the other I would be nothing. The press always make out that I'm the wild one, and they're all quiet, but it's not true. I've got some stories about Brian that you wouldn't believe."
Freddie (1985)

"We're pretty proud of what we've done as a whole. We took chances. Some of the things we did set the world alight, and some didn't. But at least we made our own mistakes. We did what we wanted to do."
Brian (1989)

"It's not the money anywhere, it's the thought of 'Christ, what would we do if we ended it?' Obviously we could all have our solo careers and put new bands together, but that would be like climbing Mount Everest again. Queen is what we do; it's what we're used to. But we'll only do it while the enthusiasm's there: obviously if people stopped buying our records we'd knock it on the head pretty quickly."
Roger

"If you have four very different people in a band like us, they all want to go off at different tangents and that's very hard. The break-up of a band normally comes from the fact that one ego seems to shoot too far ahead and then just can't get back, so the band splits up. We sort of manage to keep our egos in control one way or another; but that doesn't mean we're all so boring that we agree on everything. We've come close to breaking up so many times."
Freddie (1989)

"Music by democracy just can't be… you can't go round and ask everyone if what you're doing is okay."
Brian (1989)

"You just have to subjugate egos and you have to put the band first, before yourself, before your private life. Total faith and loyalty to the band is the thing that you need. Also, we've managed to develop our songwriting so all four really do contribute to the record. I think there's very few bands who are democratic enough to do that."
Roger (1989)

"We think that groups break up if members don't get the chance to express themselves individually. We tend to allow ourselves that freedom, so that when we come together, we can inject new energy into the group, and it works very well. At the moment the time scale for each album seems to be longer than it used to be. When we take a break, it seems to be for

a couple of years, but at the moment we've got more energy than we've had for years, so it's great."
Brian (1989)

"Without wishing to pun, it's a miracle we're still together, we've been through such change. Sometimes you think you're in hell, and sometimes you think you've seen God. If you live life to the full it is that extreme."
Brian (1989)

"We still seem to be breaking new ground, and taking chances in the studio, which I like. The process of evaluation of each other, by each other, is a big spur in the creative process. I think the group format, when it's working well, is unbeatable."
Brian (1989)

"We're very supportive of each other now. The group tends to be the most stable family we've got, although it's hard to see how we've stayed together all this time. Roger is the most extreme in extravagance and rock'n'roll lifestyle. Freddie is a mystery, nobody ever knows quite where he's coming from. John too, the archetypal bass player – he can be incredibly considerate and inexplicably rude, make someone curl up and die with a couple of sentences. He's very strange, but he's the leader on the business side, studies the stock market, understands the deals. And me, I think the others would tell you I'm the most pig-headed member of the band and I can see it in myself. Get an idea and I can be so intense. It's not good. I have to check myself."
Brian (1991)

"We were quite excessive, but in a fairly harmless way. I don't think we ever did anyone a great disservice."
Brian (1991)

Solo Projects

"I've got some old sci-fi books and magazines which I browse through from time to time. Maybe there are things up there in space watching us. I wouldn't find that surprising at all."

Roger

"(Producer) Robin Cable was doing this thing which was a re-creation of the Phil Spector sound, and he was very keen for Freddie to be vocalist. Once Freddie was in there, he suggested that it should have some of my guitar work in this instrumental space they'd left blank, after they'd tried to do it with synthesizers, but it didn't seem to be working out too well, so I did a solo, although I didn't play the acoustic guitars which are crashing throughout. They also used Roger to do some percussion overdubs, like the maraca and tambourines.

"I thought it was a good piece of work, and it was done before we'd finished our own LP, so it was put out under the name of Larry Lurex, which was a joke that unfortunately backfired: a lot of people took exception to the fact that we seemed to be taking the mickey out of Gary Glitter, so a lot of people refused to play it because of that."
Brian on Larry Lurex

"There were certain things I wanted to do which weren't within the Queen format; in a way it's like flushing out your system, and until you've done it you just don't feel fulfilled. If I get more ideas for songs I might eventually do another solo thing, but Queen would always get priority. The title 'Fun In Space' doesn't mean that the album should be regarded as 'Son Of Flash Gordon', but in many ways it is nostalgic, capturing the old days when life was perhaps a little more uncertain. I've got some old sci-fi books and magazines which I browse through from time to time. Maybe there are things up there in space watching us. I wouldn't find that surprising at all."
Roger (1981)

"I'd like to release something with Michael (Jackson) because he is a really marvellous person to work with. It's all a question of time because we never seem to be together at the same time. Just think, I could have been on 'Thriller'. Think of the royalties I've missed out on. Michael has been a friend of ours for a long time. He's been to our shows and enjoyed them. We make a great team."
Freddie (1982)

"Def Leppard's show was one of the highest energy things I've ever seen. They destroyed the place. I went back and told them so, and they invited me to play with them the next night. I was highly flattered, so I went on and played a song with them at the end which was great fun."
Brian (1983)

"To be honest, I didn't even know if I could play with other musicians. I had been so long with Queen I thought, 'What kind of musician am I?' I had been working the machine but maybe I have become too much a slave of it?"
Brian on 'Star Fleet Project'

"It seemed very indulgent putting out a long jam, but having listened to it I think it's worthwhile… it's rock blues with all the mistakes left in."
Brian on 'Bluesbreaker', the centrepiece of 'Star Fleet'

"It's probably brought us closer together and will enhance our careers. It's like painting a picture. You have to step away from it to see what it's like. I'm stepping away from Queen and I think it's going to give everybody a shot in the arm.

"But I'll be working with Queen again. No doubt about that. Queen are gonna come back even bigger."
Freddie on 'Mr Bad Guy'

"It's very beat-orientated. It's just something I've wanted to do for a long time. I think it's a very natural album and I hope people will like my voice."
Freddie on 'Mr Bad Guy'

"I was pleased with it. I was also pleased with my voice. I like it husky. It's all the smoking. That's why I smoke – to get that husky voice."
Freddie on 'Mr Bad Guy'

"We're not so much a group anymore. We're four individuals that work together as Queen, but our working together as Queen is actually taking up less and less of our time. I went spare, really, because we were doing so little. I got really bored, and I actually got quite depressed."
John (1985)

"I could hear this anger in her speaking voice and that's what I wanted to record.

"She's really what I suspected all along - a very rock'n'roll person. She's come up the same way that Queen have come up… she's fought every inch of the way. She's on her own and she's had nothing but her own belief for 20 years. She has that balls. That upbringing makes you want to scream and shout a bit and make a noise."
Brian (1987) on Anita Dobson

"I don't know how Queen fans will react to this. I'll have to find out. It is a bit of a thingy… you can't put it under a label, can you? The worst thing they can call it is 'rock opera', which is so boring actually.

"It's so ridiculous when you think about it - her and me together. But if we have something musically together, it doesn't matter what we look like or where we come from.

"I just thought, and still think, that she has a marvellous voice and on Spanish television about a year and a half ago I happened to mention it and she came to hear it and she called me up and said 'Let's try to do something, see if we can musically get something together'. So we met in Barcelona and the story unfolds from there.

"I just liked her voice. Whether it be opera or whatever, I just think she has this remarkable voice. And I was willing just to go on liking it, never thinking she'd ask me to sing with her. Then it was, Oh my God!"
Freddie on Montserrat Caballé (1988)

think we produced an album which strides across the two worlds in which we live. There's a certain amount of rock influence, and a certain amount of show influence. Again, it's not something which is instantly commercial, as you're not sure who your audience is. Most of Anita's audience may have thought it was getting too heavy, and most of those in my world thought, 'What the hell's he doing?' with someone who's really only a showtime singer. But you can only judge things by how you see them yourself, and I stand by both projects as being very worthwhile."
Brian (1989)

"It's a real strain doing solo projects, because you are on your own. You can bring in other musicians, but it's not like being in a group situation where the responsibility is shared. At the end of the day, I'm left sitting in the studio with an engineer, saying 'Is this worth anything or not?' and it's very hard to make those judgements. Most of what I like is spontaneous, and most of the songs I write, I like in a very rough form, so they don't sound as if they've been produced.

"So these solo tracks are difficult to take to record companies, because there is no obvious hit, and the material is not produced to sound like Queen records. Left to my own devices, I like to do things which are quite off the beaten track... then I wonder why they aren't hits! It's basically my own fault because I don't like the 'hit' format."
Brian (1989)

"The (solo) record is already three quarters ready. As soon as I find the time, I'll finish it and release it.

"I also produced several albums by other bands during the last few years and tried my luck as a bass-player on the side. When bands like Black Sabbath, for example, ask me whether I want to work on their albums, I still enjoy doing that, although I'm no session musician. Queen is and will stay the main thing in my life, even though I'll be working on my solo album simultaneously.

"Of course there will be a few hard rock

"Most of the time I've been working on my own. The solo project is mainly about getting all the stuff I've had in my head onto tape, but I've found that some of my ideas I had in mind for solo work have ended up on the Queen album. I think that the best ideas should really be concentrated towards the group, because it's still the best vehicle I can find - as the group is so good!"
Brian (1989)

"With Bad News, I think we made a great album, but unfortunately it's not the kind of thing that can get commercial success, as it's directed at a minority audience. But I think it is a very astute comment on rock music and the way that it's moved over the last few years. It was recorded live, and was mainly unscripted.

"The project with Anita (Dobson) came out of talking to her and getting the feeling that here was someone with a different approach; and I

tracks on it, but also ballads, acoustic guitar numbers and instrumentals. Everything still sounds very confusing and varied – let's wait and see how I get everything together in the end."
Brian (1989)

"I enjoy doing that although I'm no session musician."
Brian after guesting on Black Sabbath's 'Headless Cross' album.

"It's always interested me how members of a group interact. In different bands you see the same kind of balances and interactions. I thought it would be interesting to explore that, and actually did so with the 'Bad News' record. While they were in the studio, they really lived the part. They weren't pretending to be rock stars, they were rock stars. They didn't use their real names, and we addressed each other in character, which was very bizarre! Towards the end, they were actually playing too well to be

funny, but luckily we had kept the earlier recordings."
Brian on his 'Bad News' tie-up with The Young Ones (1989)

"I wanted to be in a working group. I wanted to play music I sincerely believed in, that was heavy rock'n'roll, and I wanted to do it live.

"It's the challenge and – hopefully – the ensuing success. If it was just cruising on the back of a supergroup, there would be no fulfilment whatever. We intend to prove ourselves – even if we're obviously not starting from the bottom. This, including me, is a working group."
Roger on release of The Cross's 'Shove It' (1990)

"Queen is like a huge rolling machine, and we're not working all the time. I am a musician by profession, that's my whole life, and I didn't want to waste it in easy retirement."
Roger (1990)

"I think I'll have to go out on my own. I'll just do it quietly to begin with – just go out and play around, just to get the feel of it – then perhaps I'll go out and do a proper tour after that. There are a few people who I've worked with on my solo album that I'd like to go out with.

"The album isn't finished yet, but I think if I get out on the road again maybe it will give me the inspiration to get my head down and finish it. I hope so, because I must say I feel a little bit redundant at the moment."
Brian (1990)

"Queen are great. I'm very proud to be in Queen, I think they're one of the best groups in the world, but this is different, very personal to me. We intend to build a powerbase through the intensity of our live performance. I think it'll be a force to be reckoned with in six months.

"Queen fits in around whatever we are doing. Queen have come so far now that we work when we want to work, and when it doesn't interfere with other things. And that's the best way. There's no point in working full tilt at Queen; they've done a lot, so there's no point working at it.

"The solo LPs were my own expressions of my own musical product of the time. This is a

whole new group, which is going to be taken seriously, I hope. This is a whole new career."
Roger (1990)

"Hard pure heavy metal, weird acoustic songs and God knows what else. There isn't a direction to the album yet and I think that's one problem I have to sort out.

"The solo project is mainly about getting all the stuff I've had in my head on to tape, but I've found that some of the ideas I had in mind for solo work have ended up on the Queen album. I think that the best ideas should really be concentrated towards the group because it's still the best vehicle I can find."
Brian

"I thought the Queen album was going to be finished so I could use the extra time we had booked in Metropolis, but it didn't work out that way. So I did all of the Macbeth music in this little shoe-string place which I've just developed, and it sounds great.

"It's all simple enough for me to work without too much of a problem. I hate too many buttons and I don't really like getting into the technicalities, because the more you get into that, the more you get away from the music.

"It's the first time I've done the music for a play and I really enjoyed it. They just asked me. They said they wanted something different, they wanted it to be dangerous and exciting with no preconceived ideas and I said OK.

"We've done film music as a band and I did end up doing a lot of it myself because I tend to be the one who gets most into it. We did Highlander and Flash Gordon, but this was just me. Basically, I've written it almost like a film score, but you can't keep it rigid because the play evolves at different rates each night."
Brian on Macbeth (1991)

"I'm very aware that the music could be irritating if not done well and that a lot of people might feel that rock does not fit in with Shakespeare. But Will Shakespeare was into making direct contact with his audience – a lot like Queen has always done."
Brian on Macbeth

Freddie's Last Days

"I don't really think about when I'm dead or how they are going to remember me. I don't really think about it. It's up to them. When I'm dead, who cares? I don't."

Freddie, in his last interview with David Wigg from the Daily Express

"Freddie is as healthy as ever and sings better than ever on the new album. We had a party at Brian's a few days ago, and Freddie didn't exactly give the impression he was on his death bed. We've heard that rumour before too, but it's ridiculous. The reason we're not going on tour at the moment is because we can't agree on the whole process. Everything else is just a stupid rumour!"
Roger on Aids rumour (1989)

"It is true that he has been quite rough recently. Freddie is OK and he definitely hasn't got Aids, but I think his wild rock'n'roll lifestyle has caught up with him. I think he just needs a break."
Brian May (1990)

"Following the enormous conjecture in the press over the last two weeks, I wish to confirm that I have been tested HIV positive and have Aids.

"I felt it correct to keep this information private to date to protect the privacy of those around me. However, the time has come now for my friends and fans around the world to know the truth and I hope that everyone will join with my doctors and all those worldwide in the fight against this terrible disease.

"My privacy has always been very special to me and I am famous for my lack of interviews. Please understand this policy will continue."
Freddie (November 23, 1991)

"It was always a private thing with him. We knew instinctively something was going on but it was not talked about. He did not officially tell us until a few months ago.

"Certainly he knew for five years or so. He was living under a shadow for a very long time.

"He made the crucial decision to disclose he had Aids. It would have been very easy to put on his death certificate pneumonia, and it could have sidestepped everything. He said 'I've got this and there is no shame… no stigma'."
Brian

"It was hard but we were trying to support him through it. He was incredibly brave at that time.

"For the last 18 months of his life he was hounded by the Press and he was really a prisoner inside his house."
Roger

"The Freddie we knew wasn't wildly promiscuous or consumed by drugs. He had a responsible attitude to all people he was close to."
Brian

"As far as we are concerned that is it. There is no point carrying on. It is impossible to replace Freddie."
John (1992)

The Future

**"People have been rumouring that Queen are going to split up
for the last eight years at least. I've got some great cuttings at
home from people saying 'One thing is certain, Queen will no
longer exist in a year's time.' And that was in 1973."**

Brian (1984)

"To be quite honest I'd like to have a house here and in Cornwall, a house in Greece and move back and forth between them, but still be totally involved in music. But perhaps getting to that level removes the necessary paranoia that keeps you going."
Roger (1974)

"Ambitious? Oh, I don't know. I didn't want to be a great actor, I don't think I'd be very good at it. I'm all right when I've got a costume on and I can hide behind it, but I would be useless at doing something straighter."
Freddie (1985)

"I don't think I'll make old bones and I don't care. I've lived a full life. I really have done it all and if I'm dead tomorrow I don't care a damn."
Freddie

"I certainly don't have any aspirations to live to 70… it would be boring."
Freddie (1987)

I'd like to be buried with all my treasures, just like the Pharaohs. If I could afford it, I'd have a pyramid built in Kensington.
Freddie

Freddie Mercury
R.I.P.

"No-one really knew Freddie. He was shy, gentle and kind.
He wasn't the person he put over on stage."

Roger

"I'm shattered. We all feared it might be coming, but when it does, it's sad. Freddie was one of the élite few who could really set a stadium alight. Along with millions of fans throughout the world, I will miss his exceptional performance and brilliant voice."
Francis Rossi, Status Quo

"If I hadn't had Freddie Mercury's lyrics to hold on to as a kid I don't know where I would be. It taught me about all forms of music… it would open my mind. I never really had a bigger teacher in my whole life."
Axl Rose, Guns N'Roses

"Freddie had a fabulous sense of humour and he was outrageous. But when we went out in public he was very quiet. He had the power to vibrate the air around him at will, and also turn it off. He never got caught up in the star thing of wanting to be seen everywhere. What was happening in his own life was more important to him. He wasn't a big socialiser, but he threw the best parties of anyone on the face of the earth, hands down."
Former US press agent Bryn Bridenthal

"I think the fact that he was so beloved – straight or gay – will focus some people on the fact that Aids knows no boundaries. He will be missed primarily as a personality, I think, and the cause of his death will become secondary. Unfortunately, there's still a very juvenile attitude to Aids in the rock community, almost a forced indifference and a desire to carry on the way bands have always carried on."
David Bowie

"Freddie was clearly out in left field someplace, outrageous on stage and off stage. He was the band's driving force, a tremendously creative man."
US label boss Joe Smith

"He realised the end was coming and he faced it with incredible bravery. The man did suffer emotionally as well as physically. In the last few days he couldn't eat and was under heavy sedation. But he was a great fighter and that kept him going."
Former girlfriend Mary Austin

"My heart goes out to Freddie. I admire him greatly for having the courage to speak out."
Moody Blues' Justin Hayward

"His contribution to the world will be everlasting."
Dave Clark

"Of all the more theatrical performers, Freddie took it further than the rest. He took it over the edge. And of course I always admire a man who wears tights! I only saw him in concert once, and as they say he was definitely a man who could hold an audience in the palm of his hand. He could always turn a cliché to his advantage."
David Bowie

"It was so sad. The suffering I witnessed from Freddie was something I never want to see again. It was awful.
    I will remember Freddie with a lot of love and respect. He was brave right up until the very end."
Mary Austin

"Freddie, sadly missed and never forgotten."
Gary Glitter

The Freddie Mercury Tribute
20th April 1992

"We would like to thank Queen and their management and staff for involving us in their amazing musical tribute, celebrating the life of someone we have looked up to our entire lives. Thank you, Freddie."
Guns N'Roses

"The concert wasn't primarily a fund-raising event. It was held (a) to promote Aids awareness and (b) as a tribute to Freddie. The fund raising is a bonus. We won't have any idea how much it will raise for some weeks. We have no indication at all. The cheques are still coming in."
Queen spokesman

"As a celebration of one man's life and work this, I suppose, fulfilled its brief. As a vehicle for raising money for Aids charities it has to be applauded. Unfortunately, in the time between the concert and this review, half as many people as were there will be newly infected with Aids world-wide. And it's going to take more than tears to change that."
Paul Mather, Melody Maker

"Largely devoid of benefit bores, this was a genuinely fitting tribute to Freddie - huge and colourful and barmy on the surface, highly organised and ruthlessly rehearsed underneath. The sun shone, Axl Rose put his arm around Elton, the sky above Wembley rang with sincere cheers and a jumbo-sized pop spectacle was finally laid to rest. Surrender to the splendour, my dears."
Stephen Dalton, New Musical Express

"Of all those who appeared, only Liza Minelli, who led the customary chorus line of stars with a stirring 'We Are The Champions', came close to Mercury in terms of presence and personality. A reminder if it were needed that while Freddie Mercury left a legacy of unforgettable songs, as a performer he is simply irreplaceable."
David Cheal, Daily Telegraph

"It's something that affects us all, it's a scary thing and also it's a historical kind of thing, no doubt, and y'know to be part of that is quite some honour. Somebody said I might have the chance to sing with the band which was – OK! Don't ask me twice, motherfucker, I'll be there."
James Hetfield, Metallica

"As Freddie loved a spectacle, I think he would have enjoyed it. Freddie to me was the ultimate performer although I grew up with their music, the thing to me about Freddie was that he was such an all-time great performer, and that's what I liked best about him."
Paul Young

We're here tonight to celebrate the life and work and dreams of one Freddie Mercury. We're going to give him the biggest send-off in history...'
Brian May

"Today's for Freddie, it's for you, it's for everybody around the world. Aids affects us all, that's what these red ribbons are all about and you can cry as much as you like."
Roger Taylor

"First of all Brian and Roger and myself would like to thank all the artists performing here today in London. They've given their time and energy to make this tribute to Freddie a reality. The show must go on...'"
John Deacon

"It gives me great pleasure to introduce our next guests. These guys are real friends and, possibly more than any other group on this planet, they understand what Queen have been about all these years. Please give your best welcome to Extreme."
Brian May

"There's really not a lot to say. We know why we're here today, we know why you people are here. We love you Freddie!"
Gary Cherone, Extreme

"I think that concert did bugger all for Aids awareness. It probably did a lot for some people's record sales. It was just a gig for some people who like Queen and all those other bands. It was alright as a testimonial but to suggest it was gonna do anything else, and then not bother to do anything else... David Bowie reading The Lord's Prayer has set back Aids awareness 50 years."
Jim Bob, Carter USM

"I don't think the audience watching will be made any more aware. It might be a reminder. I think people are familiar with the consequences of their actions sexually or hypodermically at this point. I think it's more like a testimonial match: Wembley is a great place for testimonials, and there's no better man to have it. Freddie and I used to stay up late into the night, speaking fluent Gaelic and talking about indigenous music. I'm going to sing a song we wrote together."
Bob Geldof

"There's so few people behind the glamour who really make it as true performers. It's a very strange thoroughbred condition to be a successful musician and still be able to project it with confidence. Freddie had that, and there's not many people who have had it."
Robert Plant

"Definitely one of the greatest performers that ever lived. His ability to deliver a vocal was second to none."
Seal

"You don't get too many people like him."
Phil Collins

"For me he represents an era when people were less afraid of living life to the full. This was in the Seventies when rock's extravagances went berserk. Perhaps we're not living in that time any more. There's a glorious rebelliousness about it, of freedom attached to it, that represents that whole spirit of rock'n'roll."
Annie Lennox

"Freddie certainly influenced my use of the one-piece outfit I used for about three years in the Seventies... until I decided it was time either to keep wearing it or lose weight."
David St Hubbins, Spinal Tap

"He brought operatic grandeur back to rock'n'roll and that encourages us to get symphonic and pretentious on our own."
Derek Smalls, Spinal Tap

"Although we did not know Freddie Mercury personally, we here in the band all loved his

music very much. Unfortunately he wasn't as big a fan of ours as we were of him. So in his honour we'd like to cut our set short tonight by about 35 songs… Freddie would have wanted it this way."
Nigel Tufnel, Spinal Tap

"Quite simply, he was one of the most important figures in rock'n'roll in the past 20 years."
Elton John

"We are here to celebrate the life of Freddie Mercury, an extraordinary rock star who rushed across our cultural landscape like a comet shooting across the sky. We are here also to tell the whole world that he, like others we have lost to Aids, died before his time. The bright light of his talent exhilarates us even now that his life has been so cruelly extinguished… it needn't have happened, it shouldn't have happened. Please let's not (let) it happen again."
Elizabeth Taylor

"Freddie Mercury was such a big personality. Queen had records out throughout my whole life and it's a part of us that everyone's lost. Also people have to be aware of Aids, and we've got to fight it and be aware of it."
Lisa Stansfield